Ricardo,

Viva Cobre

My Electrician Drives a Porsche?

Appreciating The Largest Human Migration In History

Gianni Kovacevic

Second Edition: 2015

Published by Kovacevic Consult Inc.

**"My Electrician Drives a Porsche?" ® and "MEDAP" ® are registered
trademarks of Kovacevic Consult Inc.**

Art direction by Graeme Thomas Berglund
Cover design by David N. Cohen
Back cover photo by Maria Tornberg
Editorial assistance by Doug Haddow & Taylor MacDonald

ISBN - 978-0-9938384-0-8
Printed in Korea
The author has extensively researched all the information located in this book
to ensure accuracy.
The opinions expressed in this book are solely based upon the author's own
experience.
The author assumes no responsibility for errors and inaccuracies.

Excerpt from the speech
"Citizenship In A Republic"

It is not the critic who counts;
not the man who points out how the strong man stumbles,
or where the doer of deeds could have done them better.
The credit belongs to the man who is actually in the arena,
whose face is marred by dust and sweat and blood;
who strives valiantly; who errs, who comes short again and again,
because there is no effort without error and shortcoming;
but who does actually strive to do the deeds;
who knows great enthusiasms, the great devotions;
who spends himself in a worthy cause;
who at the best knows in the end the triumph of high achievement,
and who at the worst, if he fails, at least fails while daring greatly,
so that his place shall never be with those cold and timid souls
who neither know victory nor defeat.

Delivered by Teddy Roosevelt at the Sorbonne, in Paris, France
April 23, 1910

This book is dedicated to my heroes

NJ for believing
CG for always being there
RB for taking that chance
FH for wisdom
FCD for letting me in

You can never comprehend how much of a difference
you have made

CONTENTS

Acknowledgments

I was once told that learning is as natural to a human being as blooming is to perennial flowers - it just happens. Much in the same way, adolescent curiosities shape our life long desires, and hopefully, bestow some level of wisdom. Socrates, once thought to be the wisest man in the universe, admitted, "I know one thing: that I know nothing." I then ask myself, how could I, a person surely eclipsed by countless scholars, possibly present a book about the ramifications of population growth?

In Steve Jobs' 2005 commencement address to Stanford's graduating class, he noted that life is a bunch of dots that eventually start connecting. A special thanks to Frank Giustra for pointing that out to me. The title of this book is about an electrician that drives a Porsche, however, as one will read, the underlying thesis has nothing to do with fast cars. Moreover it is for readers to gain a greater appreciation for the demographic shift taking place around the world, due to urbanization, and the role commodities play as the keystone underpinning any economy.

Serendipitously enough my dots did connect, just as Messieurs Jobs and Giustra suggested they would. An electrician who is obsessed with technology in the 1990s, and consumer growth in the 2000s, unexpectedly becomes an expert in the core building block that make them both possible, copper. So the story you are about to enjoy, told as a tale between two buddies, celebrates a role reversal as the life experiences of the younger electrician enable him to share his unique perspectives with his Baby Booming Doctor friend.

It should also be noted that I spent my entire childhood reading encyclopedias and national geographic magazines. This foundation would spawn a passion into following some of the great thought leaders and economic historians of our time such as: Fareed Zakaria, Niall Ferguson, Frank Holmes, Don Coxe and the Green Metal Maven himself, Robert Friedland. Their influence throughout this book is obvious.

Life will always kick sand in your eyes, so it is a never ending task to surround oneself with heroes that act as protective goggles. I have been very fortunate to have incredible people around me to champion so many of my crazy ideas, thus I acknowledge and honour anyone who gave me a chance, anywhere along the way. This beautiful sentiment, from my fellow Pacific North Westerner, sums up precisely how I will try, surely in vain, to somehow pay each one of them back.

Acknowledgments

"If you are successful, it is because somewhere, sometime, someone gave you a life or an idea that started you in the right direction. Remember also that you are indebted to life until you help some less fortunate person, just as you were helped."

Melinda Gates

Foreword

Few people appreciate that their lives depend on copper and other natural resources. From the moment you wake up in your climate-controlled home to when you got to bed at night and set your alarm on your mobile phone, you are consuming natural resources that make life as you know it possible on Earth. The roof over your head, your car, your computer, your plumbing, your heating and cooling systems and telecommunications, chances are they all contain copper. And as our global population surges past 7 billion and millions of people in China and India continue the inevitable human pursuit of progress and migrate from farms to cities, demand for copper and other resources will only grow. I've been talking to investors about these themes of emerging markets growth and urbanization for many years. Now, Gianni Kovacevic's artful storytelling takes curious investors on an exciting journey around the world to explore and discover these trends and their unexpected impact on the resource market. *My Electrician Drives a Porsche?* is an interesting allegory of human progress and opportunity.

Frank E. Holmes

1

The Office Call

It's Wednesday, and Wednesday is my favorite day of the workweek. First and foremost because for some strange reason it's always easier to find a good parking spot on a Wednesday; a small luxury that has been in short supply ever since I bought the Lincoln SUV I currently drive to work. The average life expectancy for a female living in the United States is 79.9 years, just a fraction under a nice round 80. But if you happen to be a male, like myself, you have just a measly 76 years to look forward to. Luckily, my level of income somewhat negates the limitations of my chromosomes and bumps me back up another two or three years, depending on whose research you're reading. The point being – I don't have time to spend ten minutes every day looking for a parking space. And I've actually taken the time and done the measurements: The Lincoln is precisely two inches too big to fit into most available spaces. It felt like a good fit for my daily commute when I bought it, but skip to today, and I must admit that it seems a tad absurd. What once felt roomy now feels bloated. This isn't to suggest that it's a bad vehicle. It's great, really. It's got a handsome design and a lavish interior, it rides smooth, handles well, and stops on a relatively small dime. But since my wife and I divorced and I moved into a fixer-upper located less than ten minutes away from work, door-to-door, the Lincoln simply no longer makes sense. And if I'm going to be perfectly blunt: It makes me feel old. It's a vehicle that a married man of my age and stature is expected to drive. But now I'm single for the first time in my life and it had come to represent everything about my life that I no longer identified with. It was predictable and safe, and I wanted something a little more "present", if you will. In that vein, I'm gradually working my way up to cycling to work but haven't quite made it past the part where I actually get on my bike and do it.

Anyways, I digress. The second reason I love Wednesdays is because they make me thankful I chose to become a family doctor. While medicine is an inexact science, medical practice is still, in my opinion, an art form, and one that I have mastered in my own way. On no other day was this more evident than Wednesdays, where nearly all my duties as a physician boiled down to simply listening to my patients.

Wednesdays are predictable and serene, which are qualities in a day I have come to truly admire. Serene, because it's when my practice seems to hit its natural weekly lull in terms of foot traffic. The regulars schedule their check-ups at the beginning of the week, while those with some nagging, neglected or non-existent issue prefer to wait until Thursday or Friday to come in.

Ah yes, Wednesdays: uneventful and boring, yet perfect – my own private infinity pool of crosswords, jazz radio and those obnoxious business TV shows that I love to hate. At this point in my career it doesn't even bother me too much when a patient cancels since it gives me the freedom to kick back, watch my stocks, and maybe even read a newspaper if I get really lucky. It's bizarre really, how doing nothing in my office now feels perfectly fine, while when I'm at home I feel the need to constantly work on something. It's as if my work has become a hobby and my new home my actual job.

This time last year it would have been the opposite. I was still a relentless busybody in the office, while an absolute loaf at home. Even though I'd spend lots of my time watching do-it-yourself shows, I never actually got around to doing any, well, do-it-yourselfing.

The diagnosis for such a volte-face of behavioural patterns is quite obvious. I attribute it to the two decades I spent obsessively flipping between PGA golf and home improvement shows. It was an addiction that started off innocently enough with "This Old House" on PBS, and quickly escalated with the advent of reality TV. After the dust was settled on my divorce, I had made a rather bold move and purchased a three-bedroom, 2,500 square foot, window-happy split level done in the style of early West Coast modern architecture. It definitely had potential, but all that potential rested on me getting off the couch and doing the work. It was a grand, exciting project; the only problem was that I had to live in it in the meantime. Bob Villa would have loved it if he ever had the guts to brave the endemic rain of the Pacific Northwest.

So now I find time to relax in between patients and spend my nights doing my best impersonation of a handyman, putting all that wasted time behind the boob tube to use as I renovate my new house room by room. But, mostly, I'm still just making a mess of things.

As for additional methods of relaxation, I enjoy casually obsessing over my financial situation. The recession had not been kind to my generation. And although I was relatively insulated from the dire straits that had hit more than a few of my cohorts, I was still wary of risk and exposure. I had friends with exceptional professional careers who had lost half their wealth in the crash and were now postponing their retirement until sixty-five, some even going so far as to say they'd be working until seventy. Good grief. I also had similar concerns, but I had taken a more proactive and defensive posture towards my portfolio and assets.

That said, I knew as soon as I walked up to the front door that this particular Wednesday wasn't going to provide the tranquility I had come to expect. What tipped me off was the giant floating birthday balloon waiting for me in the lobby, accompanied by my receptionist, the ever-lovely Pamela, smiling from ear to ear.

"Good Morning and happy birthday Dr. Anderson!" she said, all atingle as I walked in. I guess I'd gotten so caught up in over-thinking my renovation and finding the perfect parking spot that I'd completely forgotten it was my own birthday.

"Ah yes, thank you very much Pamela," I muttered, thinking that maybe I did know it was my birthday but didn't want to acknowledge it. They all sort of blend together after you hit fifty anyways, so who's counting?

"Fifty-eight years young, and for that, I got you an acai berry protein power smoothie. It will boost your energy and is low on carbs so it's super healthy and I won't take no for an answer so you might as well have it now."

Pamela always talked excitedly. She never seemed to take breaths.

"Oh, great, thanks for this, I'll just go and get a coffee first if you don't mind."

"Dr. Anderson, you are a doctor, remember?"

"Oh yes, that's true, and as I doctor I'm very aware of the repercussions of caffeine withdrawal so in this practice's best interest it's always coffee first, health second."

"Sheesh."

At least the day's schedule was predictable. The lovely Mrs. Chau, whose osteoarthritis is acting up again, was coming in at ten. Good ol' Cal Vernon after that, which if I were to proffer a guess, is here due to a case of indigestion he has once again mistaken for a heart attack.

After serving your community as a family doctor for almost thirty years you learn to anticipate your patients' ailments and develop patterns of predicting what they are coming in for. There are the regulars, like Chau and Vernon, who essentially need an empathetic ear and a dose of reassurance, and then there are those who drift in every few years for sporadic and usually important reasons, either due to an emergency or from some exotic tropical bug. As I looked through the rest of my day sheet I noticed a name I didn't immediately recognize – Johnny Rossi…Johnny Rossi. Who is that? That name rings a bell.

"Who's this Rossi fella?" I asked.

"Hmm. Let me check. He hasn't come in for a few years, actually. His profession is listed as … electrician."

"Oh yes, how can I have possibly forgotten. Younger guy, I met him quite a while ago when he was doing the electrical work for us at the old house. Great kid, loved to travel in his spare time if I recall."

The day went along like any other: Mrs. Chau complained about the inflammation on her leg, but mostly wanted to talk about her granddaughter's intrepid grades, which she attributed to genetics. Cal did indeed have some acute gastrointestinal issues, but mostly wanted to gripe about the current condition of the Mariners' bullpen. But I didn't mind having an extended chat, as baseball, along with investing, was something I always had extra time for.

During my break I noticed my largest current holding flash across the screen, and it seemed that my portfolio was as resilient as ever, especially Coca-Cola, which was riding on a multi-year high. Coca-Cola doesn't get a lot of hype compared to companies like Apple or whatever flavor of the week is dominating the tech market, but for me it was exactly what I wanted: Solid, dependable, predictable and profitable. Aside from my Coca-Cola stock, corporate bonds had been the investment I'd been most satisfied with, and suited my lifestyle best. If I needed to make a withdrawal in order to pay for something involved with my renovations, it was a relatively painless process. Otherwise I knew my bonds would be sitting there, preserving my capital while providing me with some extra quarterly income. I could feel my blood pressure drop and my heart rate ease into a flawless seventy beats per minute just thinking about them.

I noticed it was getting close to quitting time just when Johnny arrived. When Pamela ushered him into my office it was clear that he had done quite a bit of growing up since I had last saw him. But he still had a youthful glow for a man in his mid-thirties.

"Hello Johnny, it's been awhile, how have you been?"

"Yes it has, time flies, I've been excellent, nice birthday balloons, Doc!"

"Oh yes, those."

"How have you been?"

"Oh, you know, coming to grips with my graying hair and other such thrills. You haven't been here for a while, when was your last check up?" I asked.

"To be honest you would know better than me."

"According to your file it was over ten years ago Johnny. Tsk tsk. While I appreciate that you haven't been seeing any other GPs behind my back, I'm still obligated to chastise you for not coming more often. Say, at least once a year."

"I know, I know, I'll prioritize it eventually."

"So where have you been?"

"Just really busy with work, and I've been doing a lot of traveling over the past few years as well."

"Just like my kids, your generation certainly like to enjoy themselves don't you? And I'll tell you what I've told them, it's all fun and games until you've got a mortgage to pay."

"To be honest I'm more worried about this ankle that's been acting up than I am about making mortgage payments, Doc."

"Yes, well that's typical isn't it? What's bothering you?"

"I twisted it a few months back on a hiking trip in the Swiss Alps and it still hasn't fully healed."

"Well Johnny, I hate to break it to you, but you're not a teenager any more. If you're walking on it you'll be fine, but we'll check it out anyway."

"Sounds good."

"So the Swiss Alps? Sounds expensive, how was it?"

"Fantastic. I go to Europe often – you know me and my languages. If you don't use 'em you lose 'em."

"That's right, you're the guy who spoke, like, four or five languages right?"

"Guilty as charged, Doc. Being able to talk to the locals adds a lot of spice to any trip, I must say. But when I'm in China my guidebook Mandarin isn't getting me too far."

"China? My god, you've travelled more since your last check-up than I've accomplished in my entire life. Now, how is that fair and how do you manage to get so much vacation time?"

"I just make it happen, get busy living or get busy dying, Doc, that's my motto."

"Great motto, do you mind if I borrow it?"

"Fill your boots."

"I just hope you're not as bad as my daughter when it comes to savings. She's only a bit younger than you and still hasn't paid off her student loans. If I give you one tip, Johnny, it's that the power of compound interest is truly the eighth wonder of the world. With all these trips are you able to have any savings? It sounds like you've got a very flexible job but you're never too young to begin appreciating the true power of the buck and the discipline of steady, predictable contributions to retirement and general investing. Trust me; I've been doing it for over thirty years now."

"Whoa there, Doc! Easy on the lectures. Of course I have some savings, give me some credit. As they say, no money no honey!"

"Alright, I apologize. You've clearly got a good head on your shoulders but I just can't help but wonder when I hear about young people who travel as much as you do. Perhaps I'm jealous. You remind me of myself if I hadn't gone to med school and had more fun instead. And I've done all alright; I was able to buy my first home in my twenties because I had some discipline and followed a few basic rules that ended up paying dividends."

"Thanks, honestly though, I'm fine. I know probably think all us Generation X'rs are hard up just because you Boomers didn't exactly give us too many options, but I'm doing pretty good."

"Oh, here we go with that old sob story, you sound just like my daughter."

"Hey, I sound a lot like anybody who came of age in the '90s when all the cheap real estate and cushy government jobs ran out. And I'm not one to tar and feather an individual just because he happens to be a Boomer, but you gotta admit it, you guys had it pretty easy."

"I know, my kids say the same thing, they feel it's going to be almost impossible to buy the kind of house that they grew up in. I'm sure it's the same with most of your friends."

"Yeah, I got a lot of friends that complain about getting the short end of the stick, but you always gotta look at the silver lining. Technology, for example, how well do you understand it?"

"Computers and whatnot?"

"I'm talking about all of it."

"Well to be blunt, not much, I bought an iPad but haven't quite figured out how to download, upload or re-load a damn thing on it, that's your generation's department!"

"I feel the same way, it is my generation's department, and I look at that as a huge opportunity. And it has been just that. Unlike other Gen X'rs, I often feel like I'm the luckiest guy in the world."

"Come again?"

"What I mean is that being in the right place at the right time can be the luckiest thing that can happen to someone, you just need to notice opportunity when it comes knocking."

"Well I'm glad to see you're so optimistic, in fact, if you're also feeling industrious I was thinking of something before you came. You see, I'm working on a new house and..."

"You moved?"

"Yes, but well, that's a long story. And long story short, I've got a new place and I could really use your help. I've been trying to hook up some fancy automation system that will control my lights, air-conditioning and so forth. When they sold me this equipment they warned me it would be a little more advanced than the average weekend warrior could tackle. I have to admit it's more complicated than I thought, so how about this, you come by and help me out, I promise I just need some supervised guidance, then, we can have a couple beers and I'll let you in on a few of my investment and forced savings secrets."

"Your secrets?"

"Hey, I've got a couple aces up my sleeve when it comes to investing. What do you say, is it a deal?"

"Ok, sure, I'll bite. When?"

"How's this Saturday, 10 a.m.?"

"Sounds good."

"I guess I should ask, how much do you typically charge?"

"There's a great joke I like to use, and it's a perfect way to answer your question."

"Shoot, I love a good joke."

"A plumber fixes a leaky sink for a doctor and hands him a bill for one thousand dollars. The doctor yells 'this is outrageous I don't even charge like that.' The plumber replies, 'neither did I when I was a doctor!'"

"Har har, don't get cute Johnny, two can play at that game." I laughed. "I'll make it worth your while, plus you never know, you may even benefit from some of the stock ideas I have."

"Sounds good, Doc, and for the record my house call is on the house, but that's only for the first two hours of consultation."

"Deal," I said as I stretched out my hand.

"Deal."

"Oh and Johnny, make sure to elevate that ankle whenever it's feeling sore, eventually it'll be good as new, these things take a few months, just stay away from anything jarring."

"Thanks, Doc."

There is something satisfying when one generation can help another. Baby Boomers like me were the bulge of people born during the global birth spurt that followed the Second World War. Johnny's generation, like my daughter, were the so-called lost generation dubbed "Generation X", those who entered the work force in the '90s.

Over the past thirty years I had met most of my daughter's friends, who ranged from grunge style rockers to her university classmates. Were their collective complaints about Boomers justified? Perhaps. However, they certainly have had the advantage of being born at the right time to take full advantage of the technological revolution. There were not many twenty-something billionaires in my time like there are today. Clearly there are pros and cons between our generations, but it gave me a fuzzy warm feeling inside to be able to help Johnny with some investment advice in turn for his help with the renovations.

2

Weekend Warrior Stock Talk

Saturdays were the absolute inverse of Wednesdays. Rather than sitting at the office watching Bloomberg or having lengthy conversations about the weather with octogenarians, I was a man of action. I had no regrets about becoming a doctor; how could anyone? But truth be told, I had always wanted to be an architect, even from a young age.

Even though I was only renovating a house, it felt as if I was finally able to live out that dream. My favorite architect had always been Frank Lloyd Wright, which is the main reason I purchased this particular house, as it was the closest thing available to a Wright original that I could afford. One of his quotes that I read in my twenties had stuck with me until this day: "We are no longer truly simple. We no longer live in simple terms or places. Life is a more complex struggle now. It is now valiant to be simple, a courageous thing to even want to be simple. It is a spiritual thing to comprehend what simplicity means."

The older I became the more the quote rang true, and more than anything I think undertaking this grand venture was an attempt to simplify my life and forget the complexities of the world that had dogged me over the last decade. The irony was that in reality it was a ridiculously complicated project.

By the time the doorbell rang I had lost myself in a box of electrical cables, completely forgetting that I had invited Johnny over to help me figure out all the wiring required to get this so-called "automation" system online. The very thought of figuring out where to hide the countless cables required forced me to release an audible sigh. While I definitely needed Johnny's know-how, I was also hoping he'd help out with the electrical in general. And to be brutally honest with myself, it was going to be nice having someone around to help me climb the ever-escalating reno-mountain I had nicknamed 'El Grande'."

I'd barely had a soul over since moving in and the place was a mess of supplies, tools and empty pizza boxes. I was definitely not projecting the image of a responsible family doctor, but the freedom to live like I was back in my college dorm room days was, in its own way, liberating. I made a hurried attempt to tidy up but before I could answer the door, Johnny had already let himself in and was keenly surveying the damage.

"Hey there, Johnny, thanks for coming by, I'd nearly forgotten and was about to run out and get some supplies. I've really bitten off more than I can chew with these renovations, which I've dubbed 'El Grande'."

"The Big One. Great nickname, Doc."

"I'm trying to boost my weekend warrior ego by pretending I'm a hands-on guy, but I'm going to need the ability to call in favors from unsuspecting patients or friends to get me over the finish line."

"Not a problem, I'm just doing some running around today anyway."

"So it's another day off for you I suppose?"

"Come on Doc, weekends are for reading, fraternizing and fitness, and not in that order," Johnny joked.

"For a globe-trotting spendthrift you lead a rather structured life, Johnny. You're going to have to enlighten me about your Zen ways. Any stories you have will add some pizzazz to my being cooped up in here all day. Come on in and don't worry about your shoes, it's a mess anyway."

We walked through the foyer and into the living room, which after all these months was still full of unpacked boxes. It's funny how quickly my attention to tidiness dissipated after the divorce. Cathleen had been a lovely wife, I can't really fault her in any way, but she was definitely far more preoccupied with keeping the house in order than I ever was. She broke stuff and I fixed it. I made a mess of things and she set them straight, it was our thing.

"Please excuse the state of this place; As you can probably see, I'm still getting things in order. By the way I was half-laughing about your plumber joke the other day. I honestly have no idea how much tradesmen make these days."

"That depends, Doc, there are electricians and then … there are *electricians*."

"I'm starting to get the feeling that you're the second kind of electrician, the kind that has found some special niche and charges twice as much as the typical, run of the mill wire puller."

"Relax, I'm not here to charge you at all, I'm here because I enjoy your company. And you clearly don't remember, but when I worked on your other house I stayed super late during a heat wave to get your air-conditioning up and running. As an added thanks, you gave me your old set of Taylor Made golf clubs, remember?"

"Oh yeah, you old son of gun. That's right, we stayed to ten at night, and you kept complimenting me on that old set. Well I hope they improved your game, I know my new clubs did nothing for mine."

"I'm a ten handicap now, and I still use them to this day. Thanks again."

"Well then, I guess I can go ahead and take some liberties on you, but just for today. Basically, I bought this new home automation system and want to wire it up so I can get all the features. But I can't seem to get everything figured out and there are a lot of variables and different types of cable for the Internet, stereo, TV, and speakers. They told me it wasn't easy but they forgot to tell me you need a PhD in Electrical Engineering to figure it all out."

"Wow, look at that pile of cables – you know you're suppose to keep them in their boxes until you install them, Doc."

Johnny fiddled with the instruction manual a bit, then walked around and checked out all the pieces of equipment, one by one. As he fumbled around the various components of modern technology, I thought to myself about how quickly they would become obsolete.

"First of all, this is going to take more than just a few hours on a Saturday," he said.

"I was worried you'd say that."

"Secondly, you actually don't need to hard wire all this stuff."

"What do you mean?"

"You should probably just go for a wireless system; it would cut down on the clutter and most of this stuff will work just perfectly. I hate to say it, but I think that guy at the home improvement shop sold you a bill of goods."

"You'll have to forgive me Johnny, I haven't updated anything in years. What exactly is a wireless system?"

"It's what it sounds like, Doc, a system without wires. Works like Wi-Fi."

"Yes, alright, Wi-Fi. I do know what that is; Cathleen set it up in the old place a few years back. So are you suggesting I just scrap this altogether and pick up a new one?"

"I'm just saying that there are much better options available, technology is moving faster than you may think. I can let you know what system I have, it's super simple and works great - unless you'll be hosting any rock concerts here. Then you'll want something snazzier."

"Nope, no huge parties, but you probably got some newfangled and fancy system, I'm not trying to spend an arm and a leg,"

"Not at all, the price of electronics, as we all know, continues to go down so, wait … let me guess, you bought this on the discount floor right?"

"Well yes, they told me it was just as good as the new stuff only way cheaper as it was an older model."

"If you pay peanuts you get monkeys."

"I know, I know, at least we're getting somewhere, boy where were you last week when I needed a consultant?"

"You could get something just as good but way more convenient. For now we'll take the savings you realized on this unit and just get it done. How is Cathleen by the way?"

"Oh, she's good I'm sure. Earlier this year we were divorced, thus the mess."

"I'm sorry to hear that, is everything ok?"

"Everything's fine. It just wasn't working any more. I won't bore you with the details because it's the same story with so many couples living in an empty nest. I guess we were just both looking to start a new chapter. We ultimately decided that she should get the old house as her work was so close by and I was commuting forty-five minutes each way, so here I am, living in El Grande."

"Well then, here's to the next chapter: Onward and upward!"

As Johnny hoisted his imaginary cheers, I realized that this was the first real instance of socializing I'd had at the new place since I moved in. It was great to chat with someone who was in no way connected to my marriage or practice.

"This seems like quite the project you've got going on here, what's your plan?"

"Basically, I've always been in love with West Coast modern architecture, I'm somewhat of an aficionado, but with Cathleen and the kids it just wasn't feasible to find a home in that style that met all of our needs. So in a way, I'm living out a dream."

"Great, but this looks like a lot of work."

"I can do most of it, or that's my hypothesis anyways, and I'm trying not to get any contractors involved. Stuff like the bathroom and kitchen, walls and flooring is definitely realistic, but as you can see I'm hopeless when it comes to the more technical aspects, such as electricity and plumbing. But enough about me, how has the last decade treated you? Are you married? Still with that same company?"

"Not married yet, I've been busy traveling and trying to figure out how everything in our world works."

"Sheesh, I cringe when I think about how much of that gallivanting money you could have invested. Back at the old house we talked about some stocks you were dabbling in, I hope you at least stuck with that?"

"Things have been, how shall I say, educational," Johnny said, with a mischievous glimmer in his eyes. "The ups and downs since the 2008 financial crisis haven't been easy but there certainly have been a fair share of opportunities."

"Opportunities? What have you been drinking? Or smoking? I can't comment on your portfolio but I've been investing longer than you've been alive, Johnny. I would say that average investors have had their portfolios turned upside down, period, and now it's tougher than ever to make consistent gains."

"Where do you get your investment advice from, Doc?"

"I've read the Wall Street Journal, almost every day for thirty years. Now with these financial shows on twenty-four hours a day I have it on as background noise seven days a week. But even then, we are bombarded by 'news' from all directions and information moves so quickly now, even if you are on top of it, as I consider myself to be, the computer traders are one or five steps ahead of guys like you and me."

"Why even bother then? If you can't keep up why not just stick to safe and steady, like exchange traded funds, blue chip stocks, or mutual funds?"

"I do and that's all I do. Remember the dot com bomb? How much money was lost due to such overwhelming stupidity? Were the tech analysts who crowded Wall Street, and the investors that followed them, really going to justify the insane valuations of companies like www.sell-me-something-stupid-on-line.com or www.this-is-really-hi-tech-so-it-just-has-to-work.com? Really, what the hell was everyone thinking?"

"I know, most investments in these 'virtual' companies went to money heaven." Johnny agreed. "Who didn't lose their shirt getting sucked into the vortex? It's funny how every bubble ends the same, and then everyone becomes an armchair general after the war. However, the best-in-class ideas with strong management worked out and ended up turning huge profits for patient, and more importantly, educated investors."

"Sure, Johnny and I'm suppose to know which one in twenty would work? I was educated like every other sucker out there."

"Were you?"

"I was reading the same thing everyone else was, probably even more so."

"So what was your big takeaway from all that heartache? You followed the herd and were dealt the same fate, so you deserved it?"

"After the dot com bust, I began investing in those ETFs and mutual funds. Not just any mutual funds, I'm talking about the best of the best, fully securitized real estate funds and blue chip products. And then what? We got hit by falsified real estate ownership, supported by the hyenas on Wall Street, that caused the largest default in credit in living memory. That loss of faith in the overall system cascaded into the 2008 financial crisis and, 'poof!' 50% of the average investor's value vaporized. Everyone I knew was directly exposed and the core of everything, real-estate, was "securitized.""

"Tell me about it, we all lived it, but never forget that in every crisis there is an opportunity."

"While that crisis bred another bubble and confidence destructor, the Euro crisis and the municipal bond implosion. Who could see that coming? Entire countries going bankrupt! Counties and cities right here in the United States. Another 'poof!' like a fart in the wind, all that value, and worse, so much investor confidence was gone. Nothing worked, not even holding crisis-grade staples like physical gold."

"Wow, Doc. you're a real live doomsayer. So what are you telling me … don't invest anymore?"

"Of course you have to invest. Personally I just stay away from anything I don't understand and I stick to the things I know and trust. Businesses that have been around for decades that sell products we cannot live without are the most likely to be here for decades to come. I buy and hold Coca-Cola and McDonalds, I'll buy Microsoft and I'll hold the steady and stable dividends that they pay and I am very confident that they are not going to go bankrupt like the country of Greece or the city of Detroit."

"Seems logical enough. What kind of returns can you expect with these kinds of investments?"

"I'm pulling a steady 7% or 8%, sometimes even as high as 10%. Best of all I don't lose any sleep and I'm fully liquid. I aggregate my retirement plan and my savings plan into one diversified account, I figure, why should I pay some mutual fund manager to buy blue-chips when I can do it myself and save the fees they charge."

"So what you're trying to tell me is that I should strive for a balanced portfolio of diversified, dividend-paying stocks and just sit back and just enjoy the ride."

"Remember, Johnny, the eighth wonder of the world is compound interest. There is a simple rule that you can plug into any compounded rate of interest and that is 72, the rule of 72."

"I've read this in books before, when you divide your compounded rate into 72 it tells you the amount of years it takes for your capital to double. If you are getting a 10% compounded annual rate of return then divided by 72, your capital, doubles every 7.2 years?"

"Yes indeed, Johnny. That is the key to investing – patience, steady contributions and no overnight get rich quick schemes. They just don't work and you'll end up losing most of your money, not multiplying it."

Johnny looked around and, amongst all the rubbish, noticed a Big Mac container, grabbed it and passed it over to me.

"You know Doc, have you ever wondered how much a Big Mac really costs?"

"Ha, well I guess I should know since I just ate one. I'm gonna guess around $4.50."

"What about 25 years ago?"

"No idea, I'd have to think about it, two dollars? Three dollars? Isn't there some website where you can find that kind of stuff?"

"Absolutely."

Johnny whipped out his smartphone, flicked his fingers across the screen for a few seconds and showed me. Twenty-five years ago the price of a Big Mac was $2.20, and in 1980 it was a dollar.

"Do you know what the original price for a Big Mac was when it was introduced in 1968?"

"I guess I should, as those were my teenage years and I was eating them by the bagful, but I have no idea."

"Forty-nine cents."

"Ok, and?"

"Do you know how much oil is needed to make one Big Mac?"

"Hah! I know how much is in one – too much – and it's probably killing me. I should know better as a doctor, but I'm a bachelor now so I think I'm allowed to have the occasional dietary lapse. But speaking of Big Macs, McDonalds has been a great long-term company, if I had only just invested in McDonalds in '98 before the dot com bomb, before the real estate collapse, before the 2008 financial crisis and before the euro and civil bond collapse, where would I be? In fact, that's a great question that will help illustrate the power of patient value investing."

"That's not the kind of oil I'm talking about. What I'm trying to say is, what does it actually take to make a Big Mac, or anything for that matter, but we'll just stick to the Big Mac for this example. You have the cattle for the beef, wheat in the bread, oil, not cooking oil, but the black stuff from the ground to deliver the products and enable the processing, and then there is accounting and so much more. Oil is a commodity, and we need all the commodities to make Coca-Cola possible, or the underlying building blocks of Microsoft, Google, all your home-improvement stuff and everything else around us. How did the core elements of the economy fare the past ten or twenty years? Have you been following that?"

"Wait a minute, if you're talking about commodities. That's trading! Have you not heard one word I just said?"

"I'm not talking about trading commodities, Doc, I'm talking about inflation. If a Big Mac, and everything around us, goes up approximately with inflation then what is your real rate of return on your 7% - 10% portfolio? Have you ever thought about that?"

Just then something sounding like a UFO signal came from Johnny's phone and the flying saucer repairman quickly checked it then clicked it off.

"Damn, I gotta run. How about we chat more about McDonalds and Big Macs next Saturday?"

"So that means you're gonna help me work on 'El Grande'?"

"Yeah, let's see how things go. For now I don't have any trips planned and I find it fascinating to see how a well-educated Baby Boomer like yourself thinks, invests and, yes, even renovates."

Johnny, who arrived with no tools, and was dressed in what I could only imagine to be painfully overpriced designer jeans, showed his way to the door. After a couple of minutes I realized that we didn't get much actual work done but he had saved me dozens of hours and countless dollars by offering the most up to date and technically advanced advice that I needed. Staring at the empty Big Mac container, pictures of commodities rolled through my head like a ticker tape and I felt like a complete fool when I realized I hadn't a clue how much any real commodities cost, from beef to wheat to the metals in all the supplies laying around me. And his final poke, inflation? Have I forgotten about inflation?

As I rushed outside to the driveway to see if I could intercept Johnny to ask him one more question, all I saw was the tail lights of a bright red sports car racing away.

"Wow, nice car, who's that?" my neighbor, jaw hanging from his chin, asked.

"Um, my electrician?"

"Your electrician drives a Porsche?"

"What? My electrician drives a Porsche?" I repeated utterly bewildered.

.

3

Financial Soap Operas

Throughout the week I had been reminded repeatedly about Johnny's Big Mac comment by a series of commercials that flashed through my financial shows. He made a point of asking me the difference in price between a Big Mac today and a Big Mac in the past. The more vexing part of the question was the second part relating the price of ingredients to inflation. I was never the one who bought the groceries nor have I ever put any consideration into the pricing of what he called "the core elements of the economy." The relationship between these things and our stock talk was clearly more than just a few trivial facts that were going to help me when I watched Jeopardy. It seemed obvious that the price of a Big Mac goes up about the same rate as inflation. Easy answer. Done. And yet I had the sneaking suspicion that there must have been some greater meaning to the relevance of inflation with respect to one's investment portfolio.

Hamburgers and commodities were not the only thing that went over my head. One can only marvel how an electrician can afford to drive around town in such a conspicuously expensive car. Something didn't sit right with me, did I miss some vast redistribution of wealth while I was dutifully tending to my patients all these years? Or did I not hear the part where Johnny told me that he now owns a big firm with lots of employees and lucrative contracts? Maybe he came from a wealthy family, or perhaps I've completely misinterpreted the situation and he's simply blowing all his profits on a car he can barely afford and now wants to start saving his hard-earned money? I thought about my kids, bless their live-in-the-moment hearts, and the staggering amounts of credit card debt they've racked up as consumers in our modern world.

By the time Saturday morning rolled around I was equal parts excited and uneasy and I made sure I was outside in time for Johnny to pull up in his "work van," half hoping it would turn out to be a classic and perhaps even a bit beat up.

Boy was I off. When he arrived he cruised up to the curb in what appeared to be a brand new top-of-the line Turbo model. I was no expert so I couldn't be sure, but I instantly felt pangs of envy, and perhaps a little bit of regret, as I glanced over at my portly Lincoln.

"Ciao Doc, you have a productive week?"

"Good morning Johnny, do you need a hand grabbing the tools out of your work van over there?"

"Funny Doc, I'm guessing you'd have a full set. You've seen every do-it-yourself show produced since the '90s, so you surely got the tools to match, no? Those fads usually go lockstep with the hand-to-wallet reflex."

"Ok, you got me there, I have a pretty damn good set. What I was alluding to was the fact that your work van … is a Porsche!"

"Just a little way to spoil myself for a job well done."

"You had a good year electrifying things?"

"You could put it that way, or you could say it's nice when a plan comes together."

"You have my attention, and not to be snoopy, but just how good is the electrical trade these days? It looks like your plumber joke is about to become a shocking reality."

"Truth be told, I haven't decided what to charge you yet, and as I said last Saturday I'm genuinely interested in learning how a middle-aged, well-educated Baby Boomer thinks. Why don't we just say I'm doing you a favor and maybe one day you can do one for me?"

"Well, if we're on the favor system why don't you tell me what you're up to these days besides traversing the globe, driving fast cars and diagnosing the impact Big Macs have on society. My curiosity is piqued."

"I follow soap operas for a living."

"Come again?"

"I follow financial soap operas, day in, day out. It's pretty hard to do that if you're punching the clock nine to five."

"So, you're not an electrician anymore? Now I'm thoroughly confused, why didn't you just tell me that in the first place? So you changed careers and now you're involved in the soap opera industry?"

"Not even close, Doc, you're over-thinking things. I stopped working as a day-to-day electrician about ten years ago, and that's when I started taking my investments more seriously. I use the word soap opera as a descriptive way to demonstrate my level of commitment in how I follow my finances. For me, upping my game meant doing a little more than just reading The Wall Street Journal or The New York Times between work shifts."

"So investing has become like a daily obsession for you, is that what you mean when you use the term soap opera?"

"I never thought of it in that way, but yes, following financial markets as a daily affair has become one of the cornerstones of my investment philosophy."

"So you are an investor now, not an electrician. Does that make you a so-called 'day trader'?"

"Not entirely, I'm just an investor like you, but maybe my approach is a bit different. You see, folks like you would call me a speculator, or even a high risk investor. But am I?"

"You tell me, are you? What in the hell are you investing in anyways?"

"No offence, but most investors, and I do mean almost all of them including you, take all their 'investable' income; retirement savings, general savings, et cetera, and place it in mutual funds or blue chip stocks chasing dividends and hopefully some capital appreciation. Which are totally logical as core holdings for any portfolio especially as you approach retirement."

"Which I hope will come well before my sixty-fifth birthday."

"What many investors totally forget about is how real inflation affects their overall returns. Have you given any thought to how your *real* spending power has been impacted in the past decade?"

"This comes back to your Big Mac question doesn't it? And how a Big Mac, and the items that make it possible, climb in price?"

"Let's address that. There are many factors that push commodity prices higher and lower. What I meant by that question was, if most things consumers buy, the Big Mac being a well-known example, go up in price by 5% or 6% or 7% annually, and investors are hoping to make 7% - 10%, what has happened to their real rate of return?"

"Basic arithmetic would say it negates most of the return."

"Exactly, so due to that fact, what has happened to your real spending power on a global basis?"

"My practical side is telling me I have more and more capital when I make my returns, but when you spoon feed me in this way my common sense is telling me my *real* spending power is being lost."

"There is a great term now being used to describe this phenomenon called 'reward free risk'. Imagine entire portfolios that are striving to have only 5% returns in an environment when real price inflation is the same or higher! The problem is most of the macro themes and ideas that protect *real* spending power are not well represented in mainstream media."

"So these themes and ideas are the financial soap operas you follow?"

"Yes, but it's not just these macro themes, these financial soap operas also offer an entirely different investment philosophy. We take only 5 or 10% of our investment income with the objective to achieve 200, 300 or even 1000% with these ideas. You probably think this is crazy don't you?"

"Sounds like gambling. You young bucks get lucky on some Internet stock or oil well discovery and think you're geniuses. I've seen how that movie ends, Johnny, it won't be long until you dribble your lucky score into big losses."

"You say I'm a gambler, I say I'm a calculated speculator, a contrarian investor, if you will. But if you want to use a gambling metaphor, that's fine. Let's look at the market as if it were a casino. I'm may be sitting at the blackjack table of investments with my higher risk positions, but what sets me apart from the crowd is that I'm able to count cards by using the tools and advice offered in my financial soap operas."

"So you admit it, you're gambling!"

"Let me put it another way, a rather more conservative method of articulating this point. Benjamin Graham, often considered the father of value investing, a man who was revered by other famous value investors such as Warren Buffet and Irving Kahn, once described the opportunities in markets the following way, I'll paraphrase if I may?"

"You may indeed."

"Graham said that in the short-term, markets act like voting machines, but in the long-term, they act like weighing machines. In the short-term, investors cast their vote by buying or selling stocks causing them to behave highly irrational in times of exuberance and/or in times of panic. That's why stocks can trade at dizzying multiples in the good times and crash below book value during times of crisis. In the long-term, markets act like weighing machines as the true value of a solid investment always comes out, sometimes it just takes time. This is sound value investing, and one can exploit the arbitrage, or the psychology between these two situations to make a profit. It's a little bit more complicated than just buying low and selling high."

"Right, thus the saying 'buy when they cry and sell when they yell'."

"Yup, who doesn't know that one? When my barber's wife is giving me stock tips, it's definitely time to sell, and probably has been for a while. If you want to make a real profit in the markets, sometimes you need to disagree with the crowd. Isn't that the gist of investing – to be contrary? Otherwise you're always buying the page one story, which suggests that you are taking your position at the top or very near the top. I rarely ever invest in a story on page one, that's the familiar market where you or I can have little advantage. I prefer to invest in the story on page sixteen that is going to page one. There is a reason they call it a 'market', as the person you are buying from or selling to clearly does not share the same investment strategy as you, or, maybe they have missed something? If you know the what, when or how, and they don't, that makes them a victim and you a contrarian who can profit from the advantage."

"Ok, I admit that's interesting, but you're talking to me like a common rube, Johnny. So not only should I be following my daily papers and financial shows for page one stories, I should supplement the time I allocate by getting educated on broader page sixteen themes and ideas?"

"Absolutely," Johnny replied. "Until you can see things in 360 degrees you're still a passive investor, and I don't say that to discourage you, it's just a fact. Most passive investors panic when all hell breaks loose, becoming a victim rather than exploiting a situation as a contrarian. If you don't follow your investments, sectors and cycles like a soap opera, by that I mean every day, every week and every month, then it's pretty hard to see the tide turning."

"Here's a question for you. How does the average guy in Oklahoma or Virginia find out about these things? We're talking about these themes and ideas, inflation and spending power, which is interesting. But what was your lucky break that led you to start following financial soap operas?"

"Well Doc, as you know, back when I was working on your old house is about the time that I first started to dabble in the stock market and I ended up losing almost everything I put in. In the grand scheme of things it wasn't much money, but at the time it felt like a small fortune. And it was also around that time I got my lucky break, if that's what we're going to call it."

"I can hardly wait to hear this."

"I was working on a project in a downtown office tower and while doing so a big shot investor – a real tycoon – took a liking to me. We would chitchat about life, sports, our weekend recreations and the most important theme for me – how to make real money. Point blank, I asked him how I could empower myself to be able to stop working nine to five. I wanted to be an investor like he was. He answered by taking out a pen and writing down five little sentences on the back of a napkin, which I framed long ago."

"What are they? I bet the first one was buy low and sell high, ha!"

"You're good Doc, but I think that's the kind of advice you pay 25 cents for. Here they are one to five, I'll write them down for you too."

1. *If you pay peanuts you get monkeys.*
2. *Don't invest in the story on page one; invest in the story on page sixteen that's headed to page one.*
3. *Get a passport and use it.*
4. *If you need a pencil and paper, it's too close to call.*
5. *Surround yourself with the smartest people in the world.*

"After writing them down he spent a few seconds covering each of the five points, boiling it all down to one simple piece of advice."

"Yesterday's news costs peanuts so you shouldn't expect too much from it and you want to find great page sixteen stories to invest in, so what was the advice that combined all five?" I asked.

"Follow high quality, world famous newsletter writers. Think about it Doc, if I want suggestions on highly prospective yet still unknown stories where would I get them? The mainstream media doesn't often offer advice about specialized fields or cutting-edge ideas nor do they offer real access to the leading experts related to them. Do they?"

"So these newsletter writers source themes and ideas for their subscribers, that – let me guess – don't need a pencil and paper to figure out the value proposition?"

"These are famous contrarian investors who are experts in their specific fields with documented track records and who have been around for ten, twenty, even forty years. They clearly lay out opportunities in a simple, straightforward manner and they know all the thought leaders and famous players related to them, placing you right at the table so to speak. That's what he meant by surrounding yourself with the smartest people in the world. You may not know them, but famous newsletter writers do! However, they are not cheap and you have to read their content daily, weekly and monthly. And you have to read it like you would a Harlequin romance novel."

"My wife loved to watch those sappy romantic soap operas, but this is first time I've ever heard of them in reference to finance. I gotta say that is a great way to explain how someone should stay current on anything they are directly connected to."

"A financial soap opera is the perfect analogy. How do you know the significance of an event or development if you're not current? It's the same in a soap opera. If you jump into the middle of a story that's been going on for months or years, watch one episode, and if a character gets killed, big deal, it means nothing to you because you have no context. But, if you had been tuning in every day since the beginning, it would be hugely significant."

"Do you have a direct example relevant to investing?"

"Do you remember when the earthquake in Japan caused a tidal wave that destroyed the Fukushima Nuclear Plant?"

"Of course."

"It took a couple of days to fully grasp the gravity of that situation, but in the days, weeks and months after the disaster anything and everything that had even a smidgen to do with nuclear power or uranium mining got crushed. Point being, if you were not current, your pocket book potentially got hurt real bad."

"Alright, that makes sense. So if one had been following an expert in that field, as a soap opera, they would have been updated day to day, and made more aware?"

"Things happen in the world every day that affect investments positively and negatively. My goal, with the assistance of my specialized newsletters, is to try and figure out the trade winds that push opportunities up and down during a long-term secular trend and pounce on obvious market inefficiencies. In order to do that, I need to have an opinion, my own opinion, not a Xerox of someone else's, and it needs to be highly informed and well-researched. I took the advice of the tycoon and subscribed to various newsletters and started to follow these expert writers, analysts and just plain old famous investors. Some of these guys write weekly or monthly, some are cheap and some are crazy expensive. Collectively, they cover most investment classes including how real inflation impacts every facet of our lives."

"So the five tips on the napkin were actually illustrating the necessity to subscribe to specialized newsletter writers." I said. "But the question is how did you find them in the first place? And how did you decide who was the best and what sectors to follow?"

"You're one step ahead of me, Doc. As I was scratching my head trying to put the five tips together, I asked him the same question. Funny, the tycoon was expecting me to ask that exact question and he provided a simple answer – if I was serious about upping my game I would need to attend a world-class contrarian investment conference. The who's who would all be there for my accelerated due diligence."

"So obviously you went?"

"I sure did," Johnny replied. "I attended one of the most renowned, and expensive I may add, conferences in the world. It was full of tech billionaires, politicians and most of the famous newsletter writers who provide the financial soap operas. Over the four-day event I was able to hear thirty of them speak during their presentations, and even more importantly, I was able to talk with the ones who intrigued me. I also I spoke to dozens, hell, I must have spoken to a hundred folks, about *their* past experiences with various writers, famous or otherwise. And then I was ready to take the plunge."

"So that's how you made enough money to buy a Porsche?"

"Kind of, you see I am the most skeptical guy in the world and I still didn't believe or trust some of their suggestions. I wanted to invest in things or something I knew intimately well. I started to document their ideas and lo-and-behold after one year, and $3,000 in paid subscriptions – I told you they weren't cheap – I found that the writers I picked were up 80% on average with their ideas. If you can do the math, and I know you can, that outperformed almost any market or mutual fund."

"Well, in the 2008 financial crisis it didn't matter what you owned, everything went down, way down. There is no way you can tell me that you or any of your sage-advice newsletter writers saw that one coming!"

"When they raid the house of ill repute they arrest everyone, including the piano player."

"Which means you're trying to say, when a total meltdown is happening the good is thrown away with the bad?"

"The whole market went down; it was an all-asset-class sell-off affecting almost every single company on the board. Investors in droves sold otherwise solid stocks at throwaway levels. Fear had never been stronger than it was during that crisis. They clearly missed the memo the Chinese philosophers use: The deeper the crisis the greater the opportunity. Rather than cry in your beer, that was the exact time to rebalance your banged-up portfolio and pick up best-in-class investments, that had been trashed beyond their book value, and that is just what we did."

"Ok so give me an example."

"I'll tell you about a string of events I watched transpire from close range while following a suggestion from one of my newsletter writer friends. In the fall of 2008, there was a company that was trading at $27 per share, only to crash to $4 per share during the height of the meltdown. The kicker was it had $4 per share in cash, plus it had no debt and, most importantly, $15 per share in paid facilities. It gets better. Even when those perceptive enough to recognize this opportunity started buying, it continued to fall to $2 per share!"

"What? It had zero debt, $4 per share in cash and $15 per share in paid facilities and it was trading 50% below cash in the bank?"

"Yup, the deeper the crisis the greater the opportunity. Volatility, as we all remember, was at all-time highs, so as Graham used to preach, this created an unprecedented, once-in-a-lifetime situation. The real underlying value in the long term, the weighing machine of value, was distorted by the short-term voting of terrified shareholders dumping their shares."

"So if I had been following this particular soap opera, I could have doubled my money?"

"Doubled? Didn't you just hear about the opportunity I explained? Remember when they raided the house of ill repute, even the piano player was arrested. This company was that piano player and it was soon realized that the long-term value proposition was the sum of the parts plus cash, which equated to $19 per share. Twelve months later that company traded up to as high as $18 per share! A 900% gain! Was that gambling, educated speculation, or, as I like to call it, contrarian investing? Or was it just plain old value investing and exploiting the difference between the short-term panic and the long-term underlying value?"

"Good example, but for someone my age it still seems risky, besides, there is nothing wrong with investing in steady, staple stocks that, frankly speaking, are never going to zero. I don't want to get caught up with all the hoodlums and hyenas on Wall Street."

"You have been caught in the quagmire of extreme volatility that has been present for global investors this past decade or so. You're not the only one because it's a worldwide reality. We've all lost money and no investor alive has been immune to losses. What investors need to do is always reassess, rebalance and accept the wisdom that when the facts change so must we."

"John Maynard Keynes' famous quote – when the facts change, I change my mind, what do you do, sir?" Was my little retort to demonstrate I was paying attention.

"Another bingo!" Johnny shouted. "It's also not wrong to be conservative, and as one grows older, you being twenty years older than me, it makes sense to reduce risk. That is why for someone like you it is wise to have a totally diversified portfolio. Steady income is logical and the more speculative type of investments, educated speculation I mean, should also decrease as one nears retirement."

"Then if I don't need the stock tips, so to speak, I want to follow these soap operas to protect myself from other pitfalls like inflation and loss of real spending power?"

"Yes, that is the foundation to give you confidence in all aspects of your financial planning. However, I also feel that there can always be a responsible portion of one's portfolio allocated to well-researched contrarian investments to profit from the longest trend in history."

"Which is?"

"The ascent of man – more people consuming more things."

"So consumption is clearly one of the themes to your financial soap operas?"

"It is not simply consumption. I like to embrace specific sub-sectors in what society can't live without. If there are going to be more people in the future, and I am pretty confident there will be, then what are those folks going to need?"

"And you have experts to help you find such sub-sectors?"

"Sure do, and I found them by participating in various conferences, and being current on contrarian themed newsletters, which are huge advantages very few average investors have. How many people do you know who will travel halfway across the country to attend an investment conference?"

"I wouldn't even know where to find the info if I wanted to. You got lucky with the tip from your tycoon friend and now I can consider myself lucky that you passed it on to me."

"Maybe I was lucky but the point is 99% of the population is the same as you – too busy paying 25 cents to read page one stories to even consider that there are alternatives. I have obtained so much valuable knowledge, advice and relationships from participating in these events that it has literally paid for itself a hundred-fold. If I never attended another event again, I would still have the legacy of all the tools on what to read, and who to follow. With direct access to CEOs and other famous investors, I now have a lifetime of possibilities in furthering my eduction, and in turn, access to future investment opportunities."

"Ok Johnny, I'll admit, this is all very interesting and I'll keep these five tips on my office desk. If I want to start my own financial soap opera who do you recommend I follow?"

"Only you can answer that question because you have to invest in things you know and understand. But maybe I can help you narrow it down past maintaining real spending power. Too bad – it's going to have to wait until next Saturday."

Once again, we didn't get any actual work done. I began to come around to the idea that investing like a contrarian was, if nothing else, at least more interesting than my typical Baby Boomer ways. Johnny's ideas and passion for investing were infectious; you could see he had learned a lot from ten years as a participant. As I placed the small piece of paper on my desk I couldn't help but wonder about #3 on the list, the only one we didn't discuss. I had the funny suspicion I was going to need a passport real soon.

The World Has Changed

Johnny had hit me with a straight jab during our first meeting, racing away in a car I could likely afford but would never have the guts to actually go out and buy. In my circles, one had to be filthy rich to throw away so much hard-earned cash on such a vanity purchase.

Then he had floored me again at our not-so-productive Saturday work session with a flurry of advice and insights on a different way to look at investments. I had been counting down the seconds until our next meeting, but it was only Tuesday. My skepticism of how an electrician could find such an impressive level of financial independence had been put to rest by his demonstrated knowledge base and the tips he had received from various sources. If it worked for him it could work for me, I thought. Since we met I had put my renovation schedule into turbo overdrive. I had managed to finish tiling the entire bathroom over the weekend, and then was able to strip the old flooring out of the kitchen in a single night. It was the only thing I could do really, as my mind was churning non-stop with ideas related to our talks.

If I were to become a participant, rather than a passive investor, I needed to consider the point of our whole conversation. What sector or theme should I follow? Johnny had told me that when you consider what to invest in, you should always keep it close to your profession or expertise. Or put simply, "shoemaker stick to your sole."

Perhaps I should become more familiar with life sciences or biotechnology, both of which would be very important to Johnny's theme of "more people consuming more things." I started to wonder if he would meet me for dinner rather than wasting another Saturday in my half-finished kitchen? It couldn't hurt to ask.

I had to admit, there was an odd feeling about a middle-aged man calling up someone who is young enough to be his son to see if he can do a short notice, mid-week dinner to talk about investing. I called him right away, before I could chicken out.

"What's up Doc," he quipped.

I could only hold my laughter with his witty Bugs Bunny answer. Were we that close already?

"Johnny, I've been thinking about our discussion about financial soap operas. I've got a couple of great ideas, and rather than waste another Saturday under the pretence of renovations, I was wondering if you'd like to grab a beer and bite instead? Maybe tomorrow?"

"Great idea. I see I've got the juices of due diligence boiling inside you."

"It's hard not to, you've turned some of my hardened beliefs upside down."

"Thursday I could do a beer – wanna meet me at The Black Kamel, that trendy joint on 6th and Main near the rail yards? Say 7pm."

"The rail yards? You mean in that industrial part of town? Sure, I'll find it, should I bring my laptop?"

"Not yet…"

That was easy. For a young and successful guy he sure had lots of spare time for me, and that's a good thing. It made sense to be efficient with my time, and his, and blowing another weekend with 'El Grande' as our backdrop and not our focus was moronic.

***

A small point of pride: I've never been late in my life, nor have I ever pressed the snooze button, not even once. In the event of a traffic jam, it can happen to anyone, but I make sure to preempt such obstacles by trying to always arrive a little early. It's a strange little quirk that has worked so far, so no sense changing it. But as I walked into this so-called trendy joint, which looked like it used to be an old butcher shop, I saw Johnny over in the corner waiting for me. It was a surprisingly packed room and most of the customers looked like they couldn't be a day over thirty. Looking around the room and surveying the tightness of everyone's jeans, I felt a bid odd walking in there wearing my usual sweater-khaki combo.

"Hey Doc! Over here," Johnny yelled from across the bar. The whole place craned their stylishly outfitted necks to stare right at me.

"Interesting place," I said as I sat down, ignoring the stares. "I don't think I've been to this part of town for the better part of ten years, it sure has changed."

"I'm just doing my part to gentrify the city. Now you can be a part of it too."

"Don't hold your breath, sipping a latté and sitting in the corner of Starbucks is more my speed and I'm not sure what you mean by 'gentrify', I just hope it isn't going to be too weird, whatever it is."

"You know, gentrify, from the French, *gentrise*, or 'gentry,' the verb for gentrification."

"Oh right, but isn't that a bad thing? I always seem to hear about it on the news in reference to some sort of housing issue."

"Some might try to make the case that you simply walking in here and having a cocktail is going to result in the displacement of lower-income residents and lead to skyrocketing rents."

"But let me guess, you've got an alternative opinion on the subject?" I asked.

"Any neighborhood in which a dive bar can attract the patronage of a wealthy doctor like yourself is doing something very right."

"But I only came here because you picked the spot."

"It doesn't matter, now that you're here, you'll be back, trust me."

Something behind me had caught Johnny's eye, and when I turned to look I discovered two profoundly attractive young women walking towards us, carrying what looked to be tubes of rolled up foam.

"Doc, may I introduce my yoga partners Tammy and Jenny."

"Yoga? Wow, of course. Nice to meet you, ladies."

The pair sat down with us and began examining the mile-long beer list like a couple of naturals.

"Yoga feeds the soul, Doc. How else do you think I'm able to keep this svelte Swedish teenager's body?"

Gazing at Johnny's stunning yoga twins, still wearing their skin-tight outfits, it was hard not to get motivated.

"We go every Thursday, you should come next time," one of them purred. "We'll take ten pounds off your frame if you give us a month."

"You should be suggesting yoga to all your patients," the other one said. "Here's my card, we'll hook you up with a deal."

"Well I'm sold. If you gals get a commission for this, I'm guessing you must do very well."

"Huge trend, Doc, huge trend," Johnny interjected, obviously amused by the scene. "And you should never get in the way of a trend. A trend is like a parade; it's very hard to create one, but when they are underway you want to be tuned in. Recognizing patterns is what following your soap opera is all about. These girls right here for example, they are tastemakers. You could even call them influencers. What they're wearing today, will directly correspond with where the trend goes tomorrow. Remember how Lululemon stock performed as the yoga craze took off?"

"No, but something tells me I wish I had … where are you going?"

"I've got a private booth for us in the back"

As we said goodbye to the Betty and Veronica look-a-likes, I glanced around the rest of the room and started to wonder if it was even safe to park my car in this neighborhood. I could only trust that if Johnny was confident enough to leave his Porsche outside, I'd just have to wing it.

"So this is where you spend your free time?"

"The best way I can put it is by saying that if you were to go to dinner with just a bunch of doctors or bankers or anyone of a similar stripe, how boring is that? My definition of a great dinner, and social life in general, is to be surrounded by every facet of society. That means artists, gardeners, business guys, you name it. Try organizing an eclectic dinner for twelve sometime: That's what places like this represent to me."

"Touché. I just don't get out too much anymore."

"Even the late Ray Charles could see that, Doc, that's why I don't have a problem grabbing some chow with you and talking about soap operas. Just don't tell my yoga partners what we were chatting about when you see them in class," Johnny chuckled.

As I laughed off his comments I thought about the best way to approach our upcoming conversation. I wanted to put myself in the arena as having a solid base. Even though I was impressed with Johnny's insights, they were still distant at this point, and besides, I've been investing for thirty years. While it was true he seemed to have far more freedom than me, it wasn't my fault that I loved my work as a family doctor and had never really been into exotic travel.

"I've been putting a lot of thought into getting a little more involved in following some of these more specialized sectors," I said. "And for me the most sensible thing would be something that pertained to my career."

"Naturally."

"Life sciences and biotechnology have been relevant for decades. Plus there's lots of capital for health. Society in general wants to live longer and healthier and there is always an increasing investor appetite for such things, that much I've learned from all those hours watching business TV."

"Great start. So what now?"

"I was going to ask you."

"About biotechnology?"

"Yes, do you know any respected analysts or newsletter writers who specialize in biotech?"

"I'm not a biotech guy, I don't follow that soap opera."

"What? That's not what you said last Saturday, you said that you went to world-class conferences and met the best of the best. You were able to meet all these investors and ask them which newsletter writers they subscribed to, right? So shouldn't you have met some biotech specialists?"

"Sure, when you pick the right conference."

"The right conference?"

"Different horses for different courses, Doc."

"So you can't recommend a straightforward way to get more involved in a sector I want to follow as a financial soap opera? Now I'm confused. Just spell it out for me. What are you, Johnny the electrician, investing in right now? Besides inflation and guarding your spending power, what financial soap operas are you following?"

"Like I said, I am following the longest trend in history."

"The ascent of man, more people consuming more things?"

"Yup, I try to follow all the themes that can have an impact on more people consuming more things. But when it comes to actual investments, I've been investing in the same theme for the past decade. And this theme will be valid, in my opinion of course, for the next ten, even twenty years."

"That being?"

"I follow, and I mean I religiously follow, the single largest migration of human beings in the history of the world, and I plan on gloriously profiting from it."

"Is that a real sector or a cute title for some kind of exchange-traded mutual fund?"

"Funny Doc, I already told you that the longest trend in history is the ascent of man. That's a fact that no one can deny. Right now there are one hundred million people having sex."

"Right, so you follow population growth, reproductive technology? The prophylactic industry?"

"Boy, it's going to take me a few minutes to explain this one, but yes, population growth is one of the pillars. However, a better word to describe what I'm talking about is demographics."

"Ok I'm going to get my pen and paper out for this one. Are you going to hit me with a bible of facts?"

"I've got plenty of opinions, but you know what they say about opinions, so let's just stick to the facts. The overarching theme that can help any investor understand a changing world is to fully appreciate the power of shifting demographics and how that will affect everything around us."

"How is this going to help me follow my own financial soap opera in a sphere that I understand?"

"The cornerstone of your newfound interest in investing should be to fundamentally know who will be the 'bulge' of whatever you're going to follow. The world has changed, and if you haven't accepted that, then that's where you need to start."

Just as I was getting excited to start my new journey into financial bliss, Johnny slams the brakes upon take off. Demographics? Population growth? How the world has changed? Last time I checked I was on top of China, Brazil and the developing world, and yes I understood that there was a shift taking place on a global scale. But how was this going to affect my interest in following life sciences or biotechnology?

"So what you're talking about is growth in China and the developing world?" I asked.

"The story of China's rise has been well publicized, and I'm quite sure you've heard from all the bulls and all the Sino-bears when you watch TV or read your papers, right?"

"It's been talked about almost daily for as long as I can remember, and for the record, that theme is a page-one story, Johnny."

"That's true. But have you been to China, Doc?"

"No, why would I?"

"Have you been to Russia? Brazil? Indonesia? Africa?"

"You already know the answer to that. No I haven't, but that's not going to make me an expert anyway, now is it? I've been to Mexico and I can't speak a lick of Spanish or tell you anything about Mexican macroeconomics."

"There is an old saying, 'it's easier to see once, than to hear a hundred times'. Never was that more relevant to me than on my first train ride across China. And I wasn't staying in Beijing or Shanghai either, it was Tianjin. That's where I first got my mind blown at the sheer level of economic activity. Have you even heard of Tianjin before, Doc?"

"No, I haven't, but I'm eager to know why it was so mind-blowing."

"Some basic facts first – Tianjin is the fourth largest city in China, located in the north on the Yellow Sea. The metropolitan population is around fourteen million, and it's just one of many mega cities in China. When I was there, I saw more economic activity, overhead cranes I mean, than you could find anywhere in the United States, and I had never even heard of the place before I went!"

"Hold it right there, the over-building of China has been well documented and the fact that there was lots of development is nothing new. The real question is what is the hangover from this construction boom going to look like? My guess is ugly and two Advils in the morning is going to do squat."

"Doc, during the 1800s France became more urban than agrarian, a feat that took hundreds of years to achieve. Later the same thing occurred in the United States and it took about a hundred years. In both of those examples their populations were previously 80% rural and 20% urban; now they are the exact opposite. Only in 2012 did China cross the 50% level, or to be more concise, just over 50% of that humungous and growing population is just now starting to live in an urban setting. Picture that, Doc, there are still six or seven hundred million citizens in China who have yet to participate in basic progress."

"But that will take another hundred years to actualize."

"Not so. While it's true it happened in a century in the US, in China – and elsewhere in the developing world, it's happening in just a few decades. China's first migration wave of three hundred million people took place over the past thirty years – the fastest industrial revolution in history. With the pace of change taking place around us, and the speed at which information travels, there is no army, no government and no spiritual force that can hold these people back. You can write that down on your little note pad."

"Got it," I said as I scribbled. "There is no army, no government and no spiritual force that can hold these people back."

"Not only are global citizens becoming consumers like you and me at a faster pace than ever before in recorded history, overall world population is growing at unprecedented levels. It's estimated that the population of the world will be an astonishing nine billion people by 2050. While it's true that birth rates have dropped in many countries around the world, what we're talking about is the next wave of one billion existing people that will join us in the consumer economy in the coming decade. This is the demographic shift of consumerism I'm talking about and it will affect every sector. So these patterns deserve to be appreciated and fully understood."

"What about the ghost cities I've read about," I asked.

"If you build it they will come. In the '50s, the United States built her interstate highway, the largest public works project in the world at that time. Before that, countless other great infrastructure projects were built across the 9.8-million square kilometers of the United States. If anyone wonders about building ghost cities they need not look any further than right here in the good old USA, a country forged on ambitious build-first mega projects."

The enthusiasm and positivity with which Johnny was spilling out all these facts was impressive. I suppose I had become rather cynical towards China's explosive growth, a side effect of the twenty-four hour business news cycle. He had used the phrase, "like reading a Harlequin Romance novel" to describe how one should follow micro and macro themes, and he was clearly an expert on China, one of his economic soap operas.

As I looked around this funky little bar he had brought me to, I started to pinpoint examples of the points he was driving at. But did anyone here know what was going on in our world? These twenty-somethings knew plenty about social media and what their friends had for breakfast but are they following any page sixteen news stories, or, did they know the price of even a single commodity?

I was reminded of the first cellphone I had ever used, a giant, hulking beast that burned your ear off if you talked too long. It was pretty much useless, and the reception was terrible.

"Oddly enough, China at 9.6 million square kilometers, or about 6 million square miles, is basically the same size as the United States, but with five times the population – that's 1.35 billion citizens," Johnny continued. "Can you imagine that in rural China there is still the population equivalent of two United States who have yet to participate in basic living standards? Even more importantly, tens of millions of people are making the pilgrimage from a rural existence to an urban one. Have you seen how that movie ends before?" he said.

"You mean the France and US examples."

"It's a global phenomenon. It happens in economy after economy after economy. It's no coincidence that populations usually settle out when approximately 80% of the citizens live in an urban setting. So when I hear stories of 'over-building' in China, I consider the demographic shift that has been happening for only thirty years. Let me illustrate this even more vividly. Imagine that you were going to relocate the entire population of the United States, all three hundred-plus million people, to the Eastern Seaboard from Boston to Miami. Imagine that you needed to fortify all that infrastructure and that you had to do it in thirty years..."

"I'd say you're crazy and that you couldn't do it, but then I know that is precisely what has happened in China."

"That's exactly what they have done since the late '70s and they will continue doing it for the coming decades. Who is going to stop these citizens from making the greatest migration in the history of the world?"

"Let me guess, there is no army, no government and no spiritual force that can stop them?"

"Can they, Doc?"

"You keep saying this started a few decades ago, what happened?"

"If you could point to a single person who unleashed this Asian dragon it would be Deng Xiaoping who took over the Chinese economy in 1979. Since then there has been almost 10% annual GDP expansion as he encouraged the entrepreneurial spirit of his people to run wild. Previous to Deng, the Chinese had been locked in the Maoist disasters of the Great Leap Forward and the Cultural

Revolution. Picture this, in 1979 there were only sixty privately-owned vehicles in China! Sixty! From the time of Christ to the early 1800's China had been the world's economic powerhouse. The Chinese were only taking a nap the past two hundred years, and are now reclaiming their traditional position. How can anyone argue with 1.35 billion incredibly industrious people?"

"Sixty privately-owned cars? Are you sure about that?"

"It's a sad reality. China was incredibly backward just after the days of Mao. However, in the past thirty years China has spent 8% or 9% of its GDP on infrastructure. No other country in the world has done that, and, coincidentally, their economy has grown by 8% or 9% annually. In the '50s, '60s and '70s, the United States used to spend 4%, or more, of GDP on infrastructure and the economy grew by, guess what, 4%, or more. Now we spend 2% of GDP on infrastructure and what has our growth rate been?"

"2%?"

"The Chinese are building it, and those people from rural areas are coming. And the cultural differences between Europe and America are hugely significant, but they are even greater for China."

"Give me an example."

"The very symbols of culture, the arts and the grand houses where it takes places, were always built in Europe by socialist-leaning governments for their entitled citizens. In America, there was always a duty of civil action or specific philanthropic initiatives that built many of the great museums and bastions of culture. Whereas, in China's planned economy, they think on the grandest scale possible, in ambitious five-year plans that lay out entire cities for future inhabitants. This is unprecedented in human history."

"Johnny, I'm not going to argue this point, it's a lot of people, and the growth is mind-boggling, but the vast majority, even if they are moving to cities, are still very poor."

"Let's talk about poverty for a minute, and I need to credit Bill and Melinda Gates for a fantastic essay they wrote that addressed three myths regarding the world's poor. Myth number one was that poor countries are doomed to stay poor. They argue that they are not and I have to agree with them. Considering that they are bequeathing most of their wealth, and that of Warren Buffett, to fight poverty, I think they can be acknowledged as being authorities on the subject of progress in developing countries. They predict that by 2035, there will be almost no poor countries left in the world. There will always be a few unhappy examples held back by politics or war, but by then more than 70% of the world will have higher per-person incomes than China in mid-2010s, which is already a meaningful number."

"What's myth number two?"

"Myth number two about the poor is that foreign aid is a big waste. Sure, it's true there is small-scale corruption, but the vast majority of funds are actually fixing major problems. The overwhelming evidence points to the fact that more and more people are living healthier, longer lives. A baby born in 1960 had an 18% chance of dying before her fifth birthday; today it is less than 5%. In 2035, it will be 1.6%. That's a tremendous amount of progress in only seventy-five years, so imagine the implications as we approach nine billion people in the near future? Finally, myth number three is that saving lives leads to overpopulation."

"That's a rather relevant point with respect to the soap opera that I intend on following."

"Let's look at the facts from their essay – as life expectancy rises, societies start to have fewer children. Falling death rates actually lead to falling birth rates, as happier, healthier families don't need to have so many children. We've already seen this happen across every culture in every corner of the planet. So saving lives does not lead to overpopulation. Population growth, the longest trend in history, has been a natural occurrence."

"The longest trend in history being the ascent of man," I said.

"Another bingo. Whether that changes past 2050 due to falling birth rates, will not affect the financial decisions I make in the next five to ten years. It took just over twenty years for the last five hundred million people to be lifted out of poverty. What may surprise you is that it took a hundred years for the five hundred million before them.

How long will it take for the next five hundred million? Perhaps only the next decade, which is within my investment time horizon and a blink of the eye for any investor with a similar medium-term horizon. And then what happens when those five hundred million people leave poverty? They start consuming 'stuff' like you and I. Any way you slice it, there will be more people consuming more things and that is the overarching theme that every investor should follow because where is all the 'stuff' going to come from?"

"You're learning all these facts about human progress on the internet right? How are you sure they can be verified?"

"The internet is an incredible resource for so much up to date information, and yes there is lots of misleading, or simply false information in the mix. To buffer myself I rely on the hard work and research of leading philanthropists like the Gates' and other critical thinkers."

"As you already know, I am not a big web surfer but bookmarking cool web sites that provide great content seems both practical and important for objective decision making."

"Bill Gates has been very vocal, stating that he wants people to spread the word about alleviating poverty. His blog, gatesnotes, has a treasure trove of facts, opinions and interactive videos that offer real solutions and logical insights on the topic."

"That is something that has always confused, and bothered me. The diametrically opposed views of various groups and organizations, obviously biased, are impossible to change, no matter what facts they are presented."

"Would it not then seem intelligent to have a flexible opinion? The single biggest benefit from following those like Bill Gates is the un-biased, solution based education they wish to provide to millions of readers around the world. Personally, I don't want to be dictated as to what is right or wrong for my family, nor would someone on the other side of the planet. When we have the same per person energy consumption as someone in Africa, then we can give them advice as to what they can and cannot have, not before!"

"Sounds logical to me. I would think that most tolerant people want to form their own opinions. And as for mandating what level of modernization someone in Africa should have, I fully agree, they themselves can strive to the future they deserve to have."

"Here is a profound statistic about energy consumption in Africa. A typical American refrigerator uses as much electricity in a year as nine Ethiopians!"

It was a shocking insight and at that moment I realized just how drastically the world had changed, and is continuing to change. The immensity of what was transpiring began to set in: what used to take a century now took place in just a decade. I suppose I had fashioned a comfortable Boomer cocoon for myself over the past years that had insulated me from all this rapid change. The more I heard Johnny break things down, the more relevant it began to feel, I knew that I wanted to become a participant. I'd never even once considered the implications of the 'stuff' he talked about. And there it was, all around us, either in the food we were eating, the building we sat in or glowing in the hands of every person in this bar.

We lived in a world where technology was advancing at breakneck speed throughout every moment of our lives. Most of the people in the room weren't even aware of the preceding era where old fogies like me had spent years fumbling around outmoded technology like near-useless car phones, and before that, rotary phones.

The progress they experienced was fluid and natural, to a point where giant leaps were completely ordinary, and you could even say entitlements to them. It truly makes you reconsider the headline grabbing data points that have always polluted the media. These data points may be financial nectar for Ph. D candidates, but front-page headlines could never derail the undeniable progress being achieved around the world.

It was refreshing to be reminded that some of the wealthiest people were unselfishly dedicating their lives to making noticeable change. By providing every citizen in the world the tools to generate their own views they were also proclaiming the world had changed, and we should all appreciate and respect that reality.

5

"Stuff" Comes With An Electrical Cord

A week had passed since Johnny and I last met and in the interim I had successfully established base camp in 'El Grande'. To get my house in order, both literally and figuratively, I first sold the outmoded automation system on Craigslist. It was the first time I'd ever used the website and, to my surprise, it had been a fun experience. I'd definitely taken it on the chin in terms of recouping my investment, but the money was irrelevant: The point was to modernize.

Through a few hours of research on the web, I discovered a series of nifty automation systems that seemed surprisingly easy to set up. There were little self-contained units that plugged into outlets so you could automatically make coffee before you woke up. Automatic window blinds, voice activated thermostats, and a basketful of other gizmos and goodies. There was even an app that worked with your refrigerator to automatically notify you when you ran out of eggs. After sketching out a plan to futurize my house, I settled on a fancy lighting system that was controlled exclusively through a smartphone app. I was excited to show off my newfound tech savvy when Johnny arrived for our next meeting, barging in as usual without a knock, at exactly 8am as planned. He was never late, I admired that about him because it exuded reliability and reminded me of myself.

"Good morning Doc, cappuccino?" He asked. "I thought you would appreciate some gourmet brew for a change."

"Now you're going to tell me even my coffee tastes are outdated?" I chuckled. As he passed me the cup, I guided him to the kitchen where I had already installed a full set of the new light bulbs.

"Here, let me set the mood a little," I said as I whipped out my phone, and loaded up the app that enabled me to fade the lights from a bright white to a warm candescent yellow.

"Wow, nice lights, how'd you swing that?"

"It was actually quite straightforward, these are smart lights, so smart even a Boomer like myself could figure them out."

"Look at you, in just over a week you've gone from the Ahab of obsolete wiring systems to a tech geek."

"After our discussion on this great migration we've been talking about, I put some thought into the implications of it all."

"Awesome. Glad to see you're really absorbing all this info."

"Let's talk a little about the sheer magnitude of this shift and consider for a moment if these people start buying 'stuff' like we talked about. Just as I went out and bought the 'stuff' needed to make my home automation dream a reality, I pondered a bit about it. Then there was our talk about the ingredients in a Big Mac, which is also 'stuff'. Shouldn't that be something to follow in terms of a financial soap opera?"

"Stuff, well 'stuff' is everywhere," Johnny said as he looked around the room. "These lights of yours are indeed 'stuff', very advanced 'stuff', but 'stuff' nonetheless. But here's the question - when was the last time you were hungry, or thirsty, or in need of shelter?"

"Well, obviously..."

"It's ok Doc, trick question. My point is that once a group of people make the move from rural to urban, from peasant to worker and on to consumer, their way of life changes. Subsistence disappears from their vocabulary and their lives begin to revolve around the three C's: comfort, convenience and communication. And in order to achieve any of those things it takes a whole lot more 'stuff' than ever before. We get a dishwasher to free up time and a television to waste it. We get an air-conditioner to stay cool and a heater to stay warm. Then later on we get other luxuries like solar panels on our roofs and newer, more modern, cars. When a society achieves their very own consumer revolution, as China and the developing world is undergoing right now, life becomes less about 'needs', and more about 'wants'. With an unprecedented number of new consumers, these luxuries need way more 'stuff' to make them possible. All that 'stuff' up here, comes from down there." Johnny said as he pointed to the ground.

"Wait. The 'stuff' down there?"

"Where do you think everything comes from? The earth, that's where. Commodities make everything around us possible; the question is - who is responsible for providing it to us?"

"Ok I get it, steel, concrete, lumber, food, whatever. It comes from the earth."

"Remember when we were in your office, I said I was the luckiest guy in the world. Well I was so lucky that I won a lottery three times. By coincidence!"

"You son of a ... ok, ok, so that's how you did it! Why didn't you just tell me you're a lottery winner? Three wins? Johnny that's incredible, are you pulling my leg?"

"Relax Doc, I don't literally mean that I won the Publishers Clearing House prize or the State Lottery. What I do mean is that I was endowed with being born in exactly the right place, at precisely the right time, and by luck or chance, I chose the ultimate profession to make me appreciate the gravity of the greatest migration of human beings in the history of the world."

"I have heard some tall tales in my time Sonny, but I have to say that one may take first prize. What in the name of sweet molasses are you talking about? Because you chose to become an electrician, in the Pacific Northwest, and because it occurred in the early '90s, you think you won three lotteries? You are going to have to spell that one out for me."

"Have you read Malcolm Gladwell's brilliant book 'Outliers'? You could say I was an outlier of sorts. But let me explain."

"That was an amazing book, how are you going to weave your three lottery wins into an outlier? I'm all ears."

"First of all, an outlier, as we both know, describes people who are experts in their respective fields, people who 'stick out'. Most of these folks have had over 10,000 hours of experience and many of them were born at the right place at the right time, like that pilot who landed the plane in the Hudson River, he had over 10,000 hours of experience. Or The Beatles who not only had 10,000 hours of musical experience, they were also at the right place at the right time."

"So how do you fit in?"

"In the '90s, North America went through a technological revolution. Most of the great technology companies of our time were founded in Seattle and San Francisco in the '70s and '80s but it wasn't until the '90s that they began to flourish. All these new technologies were implemented into overdrive as governments around the world started deregulating their telecommunication sectors, and at the same time the computer age started to take off in earnest. It was then that almost every home in the developed world would buy their first real personal computer."

"When Windows 95 was released I was one of those suckers lining up at the mall hours early to get my copy. It was the same year I bought Microsoft stock actually," I said.

"Not only did the computer revolution take place through the '90s and beyond, the wireless communications build-out accelerated. Who had a cellphone in 1990?"

"Barely anyone."

"And who had one in the year 2000?"

"Everyone including some rather annoying ten year olds in my neighborhood."

"Who built all that infrastructure? Where did cellphones work? Just as this telephony buildout was accelerating, what we then called the World Wide Web and now call the Internet, exploded. And as you know, it's often acknowledged that Seattle is one of the capitals of the Internet age."

"Which everyone in the Pacific Northwest is extremely proud of."

"We sure are. And anyone who was born in the early to mid-70s was graduating college in the early to mid-90s, right? You see what I'm saying about the right place and the right time?"

"Ok so you happened to be working in a field where you got to witness that take place, but what does that have to do with stuff? I'm having a hard time seeing how the electrician part can be likened to winning a lottery or being an outlier."

"That was the biggest lottery score of all. While it's true thousands of people found great jobs in these various fields in Seattle, Silicon Valley and elsewhere, only an electrician, who implemented both ends of the technology, could see the 'double' opportunity. You see, living directly in between Seattle, a world capital of technology, and Vancouver, a world capital of the providers of 'stuff', this electrician could put it all together to connect the dots A to Z."

"You've lost me now Johnny, what's Vancouver got to do with 'stuff'? What 'stuff' exactly are we talking about now?"

"I mean commodities – what software and technology are to Seattle and San Francisco is what commodities, the building blocks of 'stuff', are to Vancouver, a world capital in the companies who look for, and provide, commodities to end users."

"Ok that makes sense. You mean the headquarters of these commodity companies are located in Vancouver. But let's finish the significance of you winning the lottery three times."

"Stick with me. Between 1992 and 2002 I did many things as an electrician. I was not your average sparky. I installed and re-installed 'stuff' in telecommunication rooms, for Internet companies, wireless companies, anything that needed a wire in it. In the midst of all this crazy overtime, which was being financed by investors like yourself, I spent an entire summer touring beautiful British Columbia. And this is when I had the eureka moment that would change the course of my life."

"Let me guess, you realized you hated being an electrician?"

"Not even close. My work partner and I were on the top of a mountain in the absolute middle of nowhere. It took one and half hours to traverse up a logging road to reach this tiny, remote enclave of technology. A small outpost of the future set against the backdrop of wild, rugged mountains and forest. We had visited dozens of similar sites that summer when suddenly it hit me."

"What happened, a bear jumped out of the woods? An eagle shit on your head?"

"Real funny. The eureka moment was that the entire planet was wireless, or would become so very soon. We were a hundred kilometers from the nearest town and you could surf the Internet or call your grandmother in rural India for a few pennies. And it was all possible from the comfort of a climate controlled shelter. This expansion of technology happened in just a few short years, so what was going to happen in the next five years? Or the next ten? Over the course of the next generation? And most importantly, what was going to make it all possible?"

"Ok, so it happened fast. Are you're trying to say it caught everyone off guard? The dot com bomb happened pretty damn fast as well. What's your point?"

"The speed of technology is making things duplicate, triplicate, and expand in record speed. It's cheaper to fly across the world than ever before and it's almost free to make long distance calls anywhere, anytime. We are in the most thrilling period of human history, one in which we are witnessing many technologies double every eighteen months! Imagine if we took away every smart phone, iPad, the Internet, all your e-mails. This would put us back to the dark ages of 1990! Computer power is replacing brainpower and the full magnitude of this efflorescence of mankind is still unknown. If we use history to shed some light on another cosmic shift that affected humanity, just over a century ago what was the significance of industrial power replacing muscle power - like when automobiles replaced horses?"

History has always been a preoccupation of mine right down to the books I read and through the phases of TV programming I watch. In my earlier years it was sports, then my stint on the home improvement fad and lately I've been fixated with watching business shows. But the two constants have always been my beloved Seattle Mariners and history. I also firmly believe that history does repeat itself and the link between accelerated information transfer and advancing technology went hand in hand. Everything happened very fast these days and I was not up to speed. I was being exposed as a technological dinosaur.

"I get it," I said. "This wireless revolution is the 21st century equivalent to how the telegraph and telephone accelerated information transfer at the turn of the 20th century by a quantum leap."

"Yes, but it's way deeper than that. Let's use another example in history to see how fast technology changes and the aftermath that results. If you were born in the year 1900, imagine the progress you would have witnessed? Flight, cars, freeways, a man on the moon, the cellular phone! In 1903 the Wright Brothers fly the first airplane and by the time the First World War ended in 1918, each army had vast fleets of air weapons. After the first mass-produced automobile was built it took Henry Ford only a decade to perfect the assembly line. His factories were then able to produce an automobile in only ninety-three minutes."

"Even a hundred years ago technology was doubling in a single decade."

"In 1900 at the World's Fair in Paris, electricity was showcased to demonstrate how it could make our lives easier. During the early part of the 1900s the whole world became electrified. This spawned an industrial boom in America, Europe and around the world that has not stopped for one moment to this very day. A hundred years ago technology could change top to bottom in a decade; now it can happen in eighteen months or less, and all of it needs an electrician to make it possible. Let's once again consider the phone, an invention that first hit the market at the turn of the 20th century. In only a generation it evolved from a clunky thing that hung on a wall into the world's favorite, most indispensable and versatile gadget – A technological marvel so brilliant that we never turn it off and always have it by our sides. Think about it, your smartphone's computer is more powerful than the one that powered the Apollo Space Mission!"

"Change happens at hyper speed, I get that, and it makes sense that investors should follow change, but we're getting a little bit off topic here. You still haven't finished the point from your eureka moment. I'm getting the feeling that choosing to become an electrician was the most important of your so-called three lottery wins due to the fact all these things need an electrician to function."

"As I sat on that mountain top and as the revelation of this massive change washed over me, all the dots connected to form the foundation of my future. All this 'stuff,' whether it was a 'want' or a 'need', had an electrical cord sticking out of it. Thirty years ago the average US household had only a few electronic gizmos; today there are twenty, thirty or more things that we buy that do not work unless they are plugged in or powered up. The same could be said for the developing world, when people go from a rural existence to an urban one, they automatically become electrified."

"The average household in China is also going to have twenty or so of these 'needs' and 'wants'. And there is only upside in the fact that the average American beer cooler uses as much electricity as nine Ethiopians."

"Statistics tell us that a fully urbanized home in China, Thailand, Mexico, or anywhere else, has about the same amount of electronics as households in developed nations. We know this because of actual, measurable, electricity consumption. The International Energy Agency says that per capita power consumption in the United States keeps increasing, however, in developing nations it's increasing even faster because more people are consuming more power-hungry things. Most of the people on this planet live around the equator, where it's hot, really hot. So when those folks get a little more cash in their jeans they buy things like refrigerators and air-conditioning, two of the biggest users of electricity in any home. You've probably never given a second thought to the implications of air-conditioning, but let me tell you, that's a type of technology that is nearly as revolutionary as the automobile, if not more so. Every trend that has come to define modern life can eventually be traced back to the proliferation of air-conditioning."

"Right … is this the part where you reveal yourself to be an air-conditioning salesmen?"

"Doc, put your thinking cap back on. The United States uses as much electricity for air-conditioning, which is a 'want' not a 'need,' as the entire continent of Africa uses for everything. That's another little factoid for you. Imagine living in Nevada, Arizona or New Mexico without air-conditioning; it simply would not sustain modern life. The fact that we now have tens of millions of people living in the Sun Belt is a direct by-product of air-conditioning. And hey – you're a doctor, so you should know that conception rates decline with rising temperatures, and that cooler temperatures increase the viability of sperm right?"

"Well, I'd have to go back and check my textbooks, but yes I believe that's right."

"What I'm getting at is that an invention like air-conditioning has a profound affect on human life, not just comfort, but everything. And the warmer the world gets, the more the world needs air-conditioning. If we can acknowledge how air-conditioners have impacted life in America, imagine how important it will be in China and

India. You can bet your bottom dollar that if we think an air-conditioner is a necessity, so do they!"

"Let's not forget about other conveniences, ones that emancipated so many women, the household washing machine for example."

"Just imagine what it takes to achieve that seemingly simple task without a machine? We load it, press a button and then get on with our productive day. What do all those women do without it?"

"I know it has been called one of the greatest inventions of the industrial revolution."

"For the billions still washing the 'old-fashioned' way, almost always the women of the family in the developing world, what do they do to achieve this simple yet vital task? They need to source the water, usually some distance away from their homes, heat it, and in the process waste half of their day to complete this otherwise basic necessity we are entitled to. This is the very definition of significant effort with near zero productivity. Do you think they all want the washing machine?"

"Obviously, why wouldn't they."

"Without a doubt! And who are we to deny them that basic privilege and key to freedom? That brings me to part two of my eureka moment, the question of how are we going to power all these things that have a cord sticking out of the back of them?"

"So now you're talking about electricity, as in, power?"

"Where does all of our electricity come from to supply all this technology and unstoppable growth, and where is it going to come from? Ever since the World's Fair in Paris, societies have consumed more and more energy. We purchase things that require electricity to function, which requires government and industry to generate more electricity, which requires more transfer of energy from where it is generated to the consumer. As demonstrated on that mountain top, the wireless phenomenon has reached into every corner of the globe."

"More people consuming more things and that includes more electricity."

"You just knocked it out of the park, Doc. Home run. Now let's round the bases. Energy means electricity and electricity needs one thing to make it possible, guess what that is?"

"Oil? Coal? Uranium? Natural Gas? Any of those will work. I give up, what is the most important thing to make electricity?"

"Copper! The red metal is the common bond that is a constant no matter how you create electricity. Oil, Coal, Uranium or Natural Gas are used to make energy, and energy equals electricity but electricity needs copper! Fossil fuels in automobiles can be substituted, however, when that takes place, usually in the form of electric cars, we need to store energy. All these green cars need to be fuelled on a daily basis, which requires electricity, and that needs copper too!"

"And you are an expert on copper because you were an electrician?"

"Who else could better understand this relationship? And the future? What does everyone talk about these days when it comes to making electricity?"

"Green energy of course; solar power, wind power."

"And none of it is possible without copper. It's the common bond 100% of the time. If I wanted to be fair to myself and fully explore the turning point in my life, it was when I wanted to know everything there was to know about the red metal. I became obsessed with every conceivable facet related to it. So that's how I won the lottery three times – first, because I started my career in the mid-90s installing rapidly advancing technology on a massive scale. Second, due to the fact I chose to become an electrician who understood the upstream, and downstream significance of rapidly changing technology. And third, because I just happened to be doing it between Seattle, a technology capital of the world, and Vancouver, a commodity capital for those who find, produce and provide the red metal to industry and consumers."

"That means that technology is directly connected to electricity which is directly connected to copper and commodities?"

"Doc, technology has been the red herring during this entire discussion. We can both accept that things are changing at lightning speed. The point I am now trying to underline for you goes back to my moment on the mountain top, everything – and I mean absolutely everything – with respect to the technology up here comes from the commodities down there. Period. No matter what is invented, and there will be tons of new computers, applications, software, cloud networking, whatever. None of it is possible without copper and other commodities."

"More people consuming more things, in other words 'stuff' that has a power cord sticking out of the back of it, means more people consuming electricity, which means more people consuming copper."

"Yup, but just try to grasp the scope of it. Beyond the billions of gadgets that will fill the homes of those people making the great leap from rural to urban, even their homes will require that stuff down there. Let's take it back to Tianjin, a city of the future – where they have transformed a toxic dump into a sustainable super city. China and India and elsewhere in the developing world are going to be building mega projects like this for some time, and these projects will be more reliant on electricity than ever, and they will need copper, and many other commodities to make it happen."

"So you are suggesting that I follow commodities as a financial soap opera?"

"Yes, that is one of the financial soap operas every investor must follow. The PhD of the economy is copper, that's why the red metal is often referred to as Doctor Copper. But it's not just copper, there is a whole basket of commodities that you should be aware of – oil, iron ore, zinc, gold, silver, cotton, coffee and the list goes on."

"Johnny, the reason I have never been interested in commodities is because I always found them to be terribly boring. But now I can visualize how they shape our economy and impact our world. The reason you were stressing the ingredients in the Big Mac was to show the relevance of all the commodities that make it possible."

"Commodities, boring? Well that depends how you follow them, you need to look deeper, see the bigger picture and connect the dots. Commodities represent the evolution of civilization and the ascent of man. When you put them in the context of the overall economy, the colossal demographic shift that is taking place and rapidly evolving technology, it's actually a thrilling subject, the Big Mac being just one way to put commodities into perspective. You asked me what kind of sectors and writers to subscribe to as you begin your financial soap operas. Your suggestion was biotechnology or life sciences, both being great choices. However, for a building block to sound investment acumen I'll hook you up with the daily soap opera I follow every day. It's a well-written six or seven pages, delivered every morning before the market opens that touches on politics, currencies, stock markets, commodities and current events. Following this daily financial soap opera will give you the macro knowledge you'll need as you identify the actual sectors you are going to follow. We'll call this the foundation to your investment knowledge base. It's not cheap but it is well worth it."

I prided myself on being a student of history, but I now felt I had overlooked a strong undercurrent that had been bubbling beneath us since the dawn of electricity. The world had changed, and technology never stops to catch its breath. From Edison's light bulb to the specialized lighting in my kitchen and everything in between, there was one theme that tied it altogether, and it was very heavy and deep underground.

I was already spending a couple hours a day reading my usual newspapers so I didn't see any reason to repel Johnny's advice to start following this daily newsletter he recommended. If I was going to make a real effort to change my investing philosophy I needed the best information available and it was going to cost more than peanuts. I was going to become a financial soap opera junky and it was going to start by accepting that Doctor Copper was the PhD of the economy and that everything from up here truly did come from down there.

6

The Spending Class

It had been just over a month since I first started meeting with Johnny and I was pleasantly surprised at how much it had already impacted my daily routine. Rather than wake up and flip on the white noise of rolling business news, I now awoke to a fresh daily newsletter in my inbox, updating the various subplots of our financial world and most of the current events going on. Given the price, and it was pricey, I had been skeptical of subscribing to it at first, but after the first week it had provided more intel, and dare I say entertainment, than I would have received from anything in my prior routine.

The most important takeaway from our last two meetings was the fact that by 2050 there will be nine billion people sharing our planet's finite resources. Over and above that, and for those who think falling birth rates will affect future population growth, is the one billion or so existing human beings that were about to become consumers. If a youthful electrician can have an epiphany on the top of a mountain that permanently changes the course of his life, then could a middle-aged doctor like me clue into the ramifications of the largest migration of human beings in the history of the world, and attempt to gloriously profit from it? It was worth a shot.

Another collateral benefit I was already realizing was my broader understanding of green energy. I'd ordered a set of solar panels to install on my rooftop that would go some way in powering my various appliances and home automation system. As a result, my dream of building my very own interpretation of a Frank Lloyd Wright classic, with modern touches, had become that more real.

I had scheduled a day off and even though it was only 7:00 am, I had already devoured today's newsletter and was eagerly awaiting Johnny's arrival. He'd offered me a chance to take his Porsche out for a spin and told me to wear something comfortable in case we go for a walk. Just as I put on my windbreaker that I usually wore to golf, I heard two honks from his Teutonic devil, and went outside to find him waiting with a surprisingly alert grin on his face.

"Mornin' Doc, we'll get our coffee at our first stop, it's never a good idea to place boiling hot liquids in front of your face while attempting turns that pull a G or 2 of force."

"Cute, a little spin doesn't mean a Formula 1 lap. Remember Johnny, I've still got kids and a business that rely on me. You know, little things called responsibilities."

After I jumped in and buckled up I was surprised how roomy and comfortable this modern sports car was. I remembered a friend in college who drove his father's earlier edition that was a far cry from the efficient monument of decadence we were about to test. As usual, Johnny got right into our topic du jour.

"We've covered a lot of material over the past couple meetings and I thought it would be a great time to recap the main theme of demographics and more people consuming more things in a little more detail."

"The granddaddy of all migrations currently underway."

"Tens of millions of people entering the world of consumerism like you and me," he said, as he smoothly peeled back out my driveway and into the street.

"I'm still skeptical on that one Johnny. No matter what they do there is no way that they become middle-class just by moving to an urban setting. Even you admit it takes decades for that to fully happen."

"Does it? And by middle class what do you mean Doc?"

"Exactly what it says. It's self explanatory. By the time these roaming hoards actually have the earning power of a true middle class, decades will pass by."

"First of all you need to get that word out of your vocabulary. The more relevant word is 'the spending class', and the real question you should be asking is - what is their economic footprint? You may be surprised."

"By spending class, are you suggesting a new class somewhere between middle class and pardon the expression, lower class?"

"Not at all. The spending class is the new wave of consumers. We already talked about the sheer numbers of people that have left poverty and will continue to do so. What I'm talking about now is when those folks become bona fide consumers or as I say, a spending class. They are nowhere close to having the earning power of the average American, but they have a similar economic footprint. For example, when someone in Thailand drives a Toyota 500 kilometers, it takes the exact same amount of gasoline as someone in Ohio driving the same car."

"No kidding."

"And when they want air-conditioning and power windows it takes the exact same amount of copper to achieve those functions whether the Toyota is built and purchased in Asia or the United States. That's what I mean when I say economic footprint."

"So an economic footprint means the fallout of when these spending-class folks – or anyone for that matter – buys anything? How big is this spending class?"

"First you need to put it into a local perspective to give plausibility to a real estimated number. For that we can use your antiquated idea of a middle class as the multiplier. For illustrative purposes let's use the United States, which has a large population and the biggest per capita middle class in the world. How many people live in the United States?"

"Just over three hundred million."

"Exactly. I have found that the best way to measure the middle class, and by default the spending class, is by understanding automobile sales. Up until the 2008 financial crisis, the United States was the largest market for automobile sales, by far, of any country in the world. And that makes sense because it has the largest middle class. Agreed?"

"No argument here."

"Ok, well if that has been established, how many new cars were sold to sustain this large middle class on an annual basis? The answer is between fourteen and sixteen million, from the mid-90s up until the 2008 economic crisis, which crushed new car sales for the obvious reason, lack of consumer confidence. It can then be considered with a high degree of confidence that it takes approximately fifteen million new car sales each year to sustain a middle class population of approximately three hundred million. Cars do not last forever, as we know, so that is a reliable example to demonstrate the spending power of a middle class."

"I'll give you that, but do those per capita percentages work in other developing nations?"

"And then some, but more importantly they can offer clues as to how big the actual spending class, those with real spending power, is in any society. Remember those cars don't care how much income you have, but they do bestow the same economic footprint every time they are purchased. I once asked a group of executives, most of whom were very bearish on China and the developing world, how large the middle class in China was. I couldn't use my term, the spending class, because that would have been a whole different discussion."

"And what was their answer? You've already given me the clues so I know the right answer is probably a ratio used in the formula. Fifteen million cars sold annually sustains approximately a spending class population of 300 million, right?"

"Very good, now all you need to know is how many cars are sold in China each year and you'll have your rough answer. And remember that in 1979 when Deng Xiaoping took over the Chinese economy there were sixty privately-owned cars in the whole country."

"What were the typical answers from your executive friends?

"I'll get to that, but we should underline this reality – we already know that China is the same size, geographically speaking, as the United States, right?"

"Yes, we covered that; around 9.6 million square kilometers."

"And you also know that China's GDP has grown almost 10% on average since 1979?"

"We glazed over that, I know it's dropped in recent years but it's still way higher than the United States and most of the developed world."

"If you saw a map of China could you name, or even better, simply locate five different cities?"

"Not likely."

"Precisely. And most other passive investors are the same. They only see the headlines on page one and they rarely look at the fundamentals of more people consuming more things. By 2025, there will be 220 cities in China with more than one million people. So to answer your question, most of my executive friends got the answer totally wrong. The only ones who were even close had actually been to China. Their guesses on how many spending class folks there were in China ranged from twenty million, forty million and fifty million people with an economic footprint."

"Ok, professor, how big is China's spending class or middle class or whatever you want to call it according to your system?"

"China has surpassed twenty million automobile units sold each year and almost every major auto manufacturer counts the Chinese market as their largest. They surpassed the United States after the economic crisis and have never looked back. This would suggest that the spending class in China is over four hundred million people, and growing by the day, and who can argue with that? Think about the total lack of awareness in assuming that the spending class, or as some still call it middle class, is the same size as a country's one year automobile sales!"

"Twenty million automobile sales in China, every year? Really, and we only have fifteen million here in the US?"

"Think of the impact that has had on oil consumption and the impact it is going to continue to have. And the majority of the parabolic increase in sales has happened in the past ten years!"

"So the basis of following the buying patterns of this demographic bulge is because it's real, they actually do buy 'stuff'?"

"You got it, and it's not just cars. Anyone can agree that these folks may not make $50,000 per year like so-called 'western' consumers, but that's not the point. What is their actual economic...?"

Johnny pauses and started mouthing a word, which, by now, I know by heart.

"Economic footprint?"

"Hallelujah! Yes! I couldn't give a damn about how much money any one of those four hundred million spending class folks earns per month or per year. What I do know is that they are buying twenty million cars per year. I also know that they are living more and more comfortable lifestyles. Textbook statistics and the nineteenth century model of GDP and gross national income, GNI, as the experts say, do not tell the story of their true economic footprint. When someone in the developing world earns $10,000 per year they are likely to spend every penny of that money on purchasing their first items of convenience. And, of course, they all need electricity to operate."

"There's an electrical cord sticking out of the end of everything they are gonna buy."

"Right, and the first things they are buying are symbols of basic wealth that increase their level of comfort."

"Air-conditioning, refrigerators and other three-C items."

"Air-conditioning is a triple whammy for anyone's economic footprint. A typical split system air-conditioning unit, the kind you see hanging from any apartment window around the world, contains ten to fifteen pounds of copper for the wiring and piping. These things are then wired to their homes and powered-up, this is the second whammy because they become the largest draw of electricity in a typical household. Finally, the third whammy happens during the hottest days of the year when everyone turns them on all at once. That may not matter to someone who doesn't follow financial soap operas, but those that do, know that there have been massive blackouts because entire countries are deficient in power generation. Even a place like Russia, with an otherwise cold climate, is host to apartment blocks littered with millions of air-conditioning units hanging from every window. The whole electrical system needs to be fortified in order to support it."

"Energy equals electricity and electricity needs copper, no matter how it's generated."

"Music, Doc, sweet music to my ears. You can't obtain this information from a newspaper because few, if any, would ever write about it. But the facts are the facts. And this is not going to stop. There are estimates that China's urban population could reach one billion between 2025 and 2030."

We continued to talk about what he had branded as 'the spending class' as we cruised out of the city and into the wild green yonder. He had driven north until we pulled off the interstate and headed west, I guessed that we were aiming for the seaside. Our discussion had centered on this new class of consumer whose economic footprint would not be too much different from the folks who lived in the neighborhoods we'd passed along the way. When someone in America or other developed nations earns the average GNI, most of that money is not saved, in fact, it is used on mortgages, rent, car payments and the day-to-day costs of just getting by. Any working-class person in America knows that when they earn $40,000 or $50,000 per year they are not wealthy, and their actual economic footprint has been static for decades. It made sense that someone whose income was far smaller, but rapidly expanding, would spend almost all of their money playing catch-up purchasing their first everything.

"So let me recap the spending class and the fuel of their increasing economic footprints. I can now see that people around the world are getting wealthier and healthier and it's not going to stop. I can also see that it's not necessarily total income as recorded by traditional statistics, but if these folks were businesses, it's more about free cash flow, right?" I asked.

"Dramatic salary escalation has been the source of noticeably increasing spending patterns, and in turn, economic footprints. I call it the Prague Syndrome, which pertains to rapid salary escalation. When The Czech Republic and Slovakia separated in the Velvet Revolution back in 1993, both those countries were coming out of 40 years of communism. They were not considered wealthy by any means and in fact you could have said they were downright destitute. What they did have, Prague in particular, was a medieval architecture-loving tourist's dream and so tourists from around the globe invaded the gothic wonderland to buy postcards and eat Bohemian dumplings. Businesses were popping up like mushrooms to feed the insatiable demand and employee turnover was rampant. Just as a new restaurant would open, its staff would be stolen due to higher wage offers, forcing existing owners to match or beat the new standards. The real earning power of the average Eastern European has increased four or five fold in the decades after the Cold War ended. This obviously has not been the case in the United States or Western Europe has it?"

"Not even close, I don't think anyone I know could boast of even a 50% wage increase over the past twenty years."

"So if your salary doubled every three or four years, you'd have lots of consumer confidence too, wouldn't you?"

"Who wouldn't!"

"The hyperinflation that plagued the world thirty years ago is gone, not one country suffers from it anymore, Zimbabwe being the last until they dollarized their economy."

"And what does that have to do with the spending class and economic footprints?"

"Recessions rob citizens of what they might have, whereas hyperinflation robs you of what you already have. In 1979, there were over thirty developing countries suffering from hyperinflation; today there are zero. What does that newfound confidence do to the emerging classes?"

"Unleashes a tremendous amount of confidence and optimism, obviously."

"All over the world this new spending class has found wealth, anchored by this confidence and optimism we have not experienced in two generations. And they are buying 'stuff' on a scale never seen in history."

"And all of it needs power."

"Same as here, same as Europe, they want the same things we have, and let me tell you none of their children are playing with hula-hoops or spinning tops."

As we finish that thought we pull into a large parking lot overlooking a vast industrial complex. I had seen this sprawling complex before but had never taken the time to soak up the scale of it. It was clear that this was our destination all along when we stopped dead center of the main structure.

"What do you see?" Johnny asks me.

"That is the largest industrial factory I've ever seen in my life."

"No matter if you're rich or poor, upper class or lower class, and whether you live in Mumbai or New York, you cannot live without it. That, Doctor Anderson, is an oil refinery."

"Even if you're a hermit and live in a solar-powered organic oasis?"

"Even then, oil refineries not only make gasoline, heating fuel and lubricants possible, they also provide specialized fuels like distillates and kerosene for the jet aircraft we fly in. This kind of infrastructure is vital for any growing society. Even if you want to drive your brand-new electric car, it requires rubber tires and you still need to charge it, and that requires electricity."

"So no matter what kind of transportation we use we still need refineries. And when it comes to creating electricity, the greener and cleaner it is generated, the more that is demanded of copper."

"That's right, Doc, and I am an environmentalist. But I know the world is not going to stop advancing. Greens can choose whatever method of making electricity they see fit because I know green energy translates into more demand for copper. Even their electric cars need ten times more copper than a gasoline engine and they still need to be charged. Simply put, traditional methods of making energy need lots of copper, but greener methods need even more. Do you know what a NIMBY is Doc?"

"Some kind of a hotdog?"

"Let me spell it out for you, N.I.M.B.Y. and it stands for not-in-my-back-yard. That is what they might as well call that refinery. Nobody wants a new refinery to be built, or a new copper mine, or an oil pipeline or anything that even comes close. Could you imagine how hard it would be to build that refinery today?"

"Damn near impossible."

"Without a doubt, so can you not see the value in the ones that are already there?"

"Let me guess, you're also an expert on refineries and pipelines?"

"I follow energy. Energy, in all its forms is one of my economic soap operas. We all need it and no one can live without it. Industry can shift between fuel sources, bouncing from coal to nuclear or oil to natural gas, but the common bond is always copper, no matter which energy source is used."

"Energy equals electricity."

"The lesson to be learned from visiting a site like this is – how will the nine billion people in 2050 have the things you and I take for granted? Does it not make sense to know and understand the policies that affect them and the patterns that make them relevant?"

"I'm ready to pinpoint my second financial soap opera Johnny. Perhaps it's time we attended one of these conferences you talk so highly of?"

"My thoughts exactly. The New Orleans event, my top destination of the year if you recall, will take place one month from now. I'm already booked; I suggest you buy your plane ticket today. And don't forget, air travel these days requires a passport!"

Johnny had used a tip from an über-successful individual to become a participant in a whole new way of following financial markets. For him that journey came full circle at get-togethers surrounded by contrarians where he was able to use his outlier expertise to offer insights into the backbone of global growth – energy. The advantage I had was my introduction was being accelerated due to my special relationship with this storytelling electrician. Converting everything I was learning into actionable ideas required me to attend the Mecca of alternative thinking.

7

The 4% Club

The New Orleans Contrarian Investing Conference was fast approaching and I found myself spending all my free time researching the finer details of attending. As I was investing over $5,000 to cover my travel costs, accommodation and admission, not to mention the five days and nights out of my valuable schedule, it was the prudent thing to do.

Aside from getting the most bang for my buck, I wanted to be prepared. I was about to take a meaningful and pricey departure away from the investment philosophy I had stuck with for most of my life, so not only did I want to know everything there was to know about what I was getting into, but I wanted to be able to efficiently capitalize on my time spent at the conference. If I was going to be a participant, I needed to participate.

There would be over five hundred different companies showcasing their assets and as many senior executives to talk to so I even went so far as to research these personalities. Over and above the myriad of investment opportunities, there would be dozens of well respected newsletter writers to listen to and a keynote debate featuring a Republican, a Democrat and a revered libertarian. I could hardly wait.

The flight from Seattle to New Orleans was around six hours, providing me with enough time for one last skim over everything I'd learned in the past months. We had covered the demographics of population growth, more people consuming more things, and how technology would affect and be affected by it all.

While it was true that it was difficult to predict the short-term effects of government policy and economic earthquakes, especially in a post-crisis world, this unstoppable army of new consumers was our focus for when we touched down in New Orleans. I was going to apply these months of hard work to try to find the proverbial needle in a haystack. I had found my first major theme in population growth, but I wanted to secure something else to follow closely, meet a mentor to help guide me with updates in the future, and hopefully land some contrarian investments. And if all else failed, Johnny had attended this conference numerous times so he was my trump card.

When we rolled out of Louis Armstrong International to hail a cab, the first thing to hit me was the heat. It was hot, but not too humid, a welcome departure from the relentless downpour that had overtaken Washington State since the first leaves began to fall.

"Your first time to the Big Easy?" Johnny asked when I stopped for a minute to take off my jacket. "I told you that you wouldn't need that sweater."

"It's fantastic, I'm finally crossing it off the bucket list I never knew I had."

"This is my favorite city in the world, and you're about to see why. We're staying in the hotel attached to the show. I always do. Not only does it save time, all the major CEOs and speakers are there too. It's twice as expensive when you book late but invaluable if you meet someone in the elevator, or better yet, swing an off-the-cuff breakfast or lunch together."

Johnny's saying, "if you pay peanuts you get monkeys", began to ring truer and truer, and aside from investing, it seemed to work in many other aspects of life. I reflected back on all the crappy sunglasses or shoes I'd purchased over the years just to watch them fall apart or break. Buy high quality once, or buy garbage thrice, either way you're paying the same but when you pay peanuts you're stuck with mediocrity.

I was especially impressed in respect to his choosing a more expensive, yet highly strategic hotel, which is something I never would have considered on my own. I could have saved money on the room and opted for the Best Western, but I'd only be getting half of the experience and even less of the access. There was a sweet sense of satisfaction knowing that I was getting a bargain by paying twice as much as other attendees for this distinct advantage.

"I'm just glad they had space," I told Johnny as our cab pulled up to the hotel, our baggage swiftly picked up by a duo of stealthy bellhops.

"The hotel is booked one year in advance for events like these, mostly for the VIPs but they always leave a few rooms, at double the price, for last minute reservations or guys like you and me who insist on being here, and they know that."

"Alright Johnny, we're going to make the best of it and I've mapped out each day's highlights, so why don't we…"

"Whoa there Doc, you're getting a little bit ahead of yourself, let's start by figuring out who we aren't going to spend any time with."

"I was thinking we were here to meet everyone and see everything."

"The conference lasts four days, there are five hundred companies and thirty presentations per day, panels and keynotes, plus the social events."

"Exactly, so I thought I could go through the aisles and cover 150 companies per day, in between sitting in on fifteen stage presentations, and naturally the keynotes are a given."

"Ok, so you want to find out everything you can about investing in assisted living partnerships? How about commercial real estate opportunities? There is also an interesting discussion on shifting tides in mutual fund performance fees that you probably want to dedicate an entire two hours to?"

"You made your point. I spent weeks preparing so I do have a short list and I don't want to address anything that is not connected to, as you put it, the largest migration of human beings in history. I was simply thinking that I could skim the showroom floor to get a feel for how it works."

"I did the same my first time through, and there is value in that approach. But when you have the advantage of accelerating your familiarity with knowing who's who in the zoo, it's far better than throwing darts at the showroom floor. Even if you didn't have me as a guide, any new investor's early foray into contrarian investing should be focused on finding out what they want to invest in, and you already know that the theme is population growth and how it effects energy, consumption, commodities and Doctor Copper. Now you need to know who the perennial winners are. I personally take a more strategic approach, starting with a qualified short list and then spending my limited event time being surrounded by them. But I always start with my 4% Club."

"Your 4% Club? You brought that up before; fill me in on the meaning of that."

"The 4% Club comes from Pareto's Law. That was coined by an Italian economist of the same name who discovered a principle that 20% of the effort creates 80% of the gain. It was later observed that this worked in many facets of the economy and in society. It was also seen that the 20% on the other end of the spectrum caused 80% of the problems and misery. Over one hundred years later it is still relevant and we can see numerous examples including our urban-to-rural migration example."

"So that's the 80/20 rule, I have heard about that, but how do you get down to 4%?"

"The 4% Club members are the top performers with respect to investing. Within Pareto's Law there is yet another Pareto's Law. This would suggest that 20% of those original 20%, which is where the 4% comes from, create the overwhelming bulk of the super successes. This is especially true in regards to higher-risk contrarian investing."

"And on the other end of the spectrum? There are a few bad apples that create a disproportionate amount of the grief?"

120

"Sadly, that's the case. George Bernard Shaw had a great quote to address that exact sentiment – he said that 'horse racing was created by the upper classes and the lower classes to fleece the middle classes.' This can easily be used to describe Jr. Stock Markets and speculative investments, or what you and I call contrarian investing."

"So those are the guys to steer clear from? And as it's hard to tell who they are, you stay on the top part of Pareto's Law and only focus on those with an exceptional track record, which is the 4% Club?"

"If I can avoid it, I never approach a goat from the front, a horse from the back or a fool from any side. Investing with fools is gambling whereas investing with those that have had four or five or more positive outcomes for shareholders is confident, intelligent investing. And if I can buy those management teams at a discount, when markets correct, then that is the true definition of contrarian investing."

"What are some of the factors that differentiate a 4 percenter from others?"

"The 4 percenters that I follow always have the most skin in the game. That means the investor that has the most to lose is the 4 percenter. There are too many company executives who are working for salary and stock options and less so for stakeholder appreciation. You and I, as investors, only make money one way, when the shares we buy and hold appreciate. Some of the 4 percenters I follow don't even take a salary! They make money when the investor makes money, a true alignment with the investor's interest. If things don't work out, the single biggest loser will be them, just the same as when things work out they stand to make the most profit – which, by the way, has historically happened more often and totally out of proportion to the industry average."

"So, for these reasons, you want us to spend all of our time following the 4% Club?"

"If you don't allocate your time to a condensed format within the overall conference, then after four days you'll find yourself confused and conflicted and you will end up with too much un-actionable information. Besides, the conference is only eight hours per day and you want to sit in on at least fifteen talks during those eight hours, after all that's why we're here. But that would leave you with only a couple minutes per company."

"In other words, running around like a chicken with no head on is not a strategy."

"What you're forgetting is the advice that the tycoon gave me and I gave you. There are teams of famous newsletter analysts that comb the conference floor for you. They already know all the players in the sectors they follow so you don't have to waste your time wooing total strangers. You can accelerate your dedication by listening to your short list of favorite writers, follow their filtered list, and then concentrate on the overlap that occurs when you see our 4 percenters involved with those picks. That is when all the planets align and you can invest with more confidence. That is exactly what that tycoon did, it is what I do and it's worked for both of us."

"You're right again. If I am going to pay someone for great ideas and information, they can do the walking for me. When I narrow it down, due to my reading and research, I can then go zero in on specific companies and request discussions with their executives. So I should spend my time listening to and interviewing the newsletter writers of interest who have expertise in my favorite fields of, consumption, commodities and copper?"

"Doc, who's teaching you? Buy that man a cape!"

It was only day one and that meant the lightest schedule of the conference and time for attendees to enjoy a kick-off cocktail. Rather than gather before the main event, I wanted to go back to my room and adjust my attack list. What was clear is that we were going to focus on the analysts that cover the companies that offered the best opportunity to feed the spending class.

Johnny, on the other hand, wanted to rub elbows with the many friends and contacts he had met over the years. I needed to reassess, and wasn't quite ready to dive head first into the swimming pool, so I went to relax in my room, enjoy a bourbon – if you're in the South, might as well drink what the locals drink – and pour over the conference literature.

Understanding who I wanted to listen to was important because they were the ones I wanted to meet. Were the other attendees going to be as focused as Johnny and I were?

With so many valid opportunities readily available, how many of my fellow contrarians were going to be fixated on the theme of consumption in the developing world? One thing was for sure, I was going to have a razor sharp focus and not let anything stand in the way of yours truly having pure and unfettered access to the thought leaders of my new found passion.

The Keynote

If you don't travel that often, like me, then you cannot truly appreciate the gravity of the term jet lag as you've probably become conditioned to it. In the medical field we call it desynchronosis, for the Latin unsynchronized, as transmeridian air travel tends to rapidly alter your circadian rhythm, resulting in sleep disruption, decreased cognitive ability, headaches, irritability and sometimes indigestion.

Basically, it takes a hammer to your internal clock if not managed properly.

There was just a two-hour time difference between the west and east coasts but the loss of those precious few hours had already taken its toll on me. As soon as I woke up, I felt the need to supplement my typical two cups of morning coffee with an extra shot of espresso, a room service splurge, which left me jittery and anxious on a day where I was already both of those things. By the time I came to my senses, I realized it was nearly time to hit the conference floor and I was furiously reviewing my notes like I was back in university cramming for an exam. To say I was excited was an understatement. I was giddier than a schoolgirl on Valentine's Day.

The only so called "professional gatherings" I usually attended were the humdrum annual Medical Association meetings. Listening to my fellow colleagues pontificate on the effects of this new drug or that old treatment was about as exciting as listening to someone describe the science behind how to solve a Rubik's Cube. The world of contrarian investing was an entirely different beast; it was an art not a science.

Being located at the event hotel provided a convenient home base to operate from and enabled Johnny and me quick in-and-out access to everything we wanted to attend. Our first breakfast served as the start of the conference and was taking place in an open and social atmosphere. The most unique aspect of this walk-and-talk format was the vast amount of hand-selected companies and executives from totally diverse fields: Bio-technology, natural resource companies; metals and energy, hi-tech and real estate income funds. There was even a group from Argentina selling a "lifestyle" community dubbed as the real life "Galt's Gulch" from Atlas Shrugged.

Intermingling with this eclectic group were curious participants like myself, authors of well-known books, newsletter writers from the conference agenda, various high-profile investors and even some notable politicians. This was a genuine potpourri of economic intelligence and investment firepower and it felt like you couldn't brush the opportunity away if you tried, and I was standing there smack dab in the middle just trying to absorb it all.

After I had milled around for about ten minutes trying not to be bewildered, someone tapped my shoulder. I looked around to find Johnny at my side.

"You fell for that old gag Doc!"

As I turned around to face Johnny, I saw a small crowd gather around some distant figure. Like a moth to a warm light, I was also curious about what was going on and so had been gravitating towards the gawkers.

"Who's that?"

"The keynote speaker."

"But it's only breakfast time."

"Every day, there is a kick-off speaker, a lunch speaker and a final panel, over and above the daily agenda. However, the first talk of the conference is always something to look forward to and this year we are in for a real treat."

"Wow, when I was reviewing the agenda last night it listed the first speaker as a mining executive, not exactly what I would call speaker hall fireworks."

"Once you've heard all the talks, met with most of the newsletter crowd and glad handed with your fellow contrarians you can tell me who you thought was the most engaging. For now I can only tell you that he is well worth the billing as the conference inaugurator."

The crowd continued to build around this mining maven. In his biography it stated that he had successfully sold three companies for billions of dollars and was always the single largest shareholder in each instance. That would suggest he was a legitimate tycoon but it did not explain why the conference organizers would choose some rock jock over a high-flying tech geek or real estate mogul to open things up. There would seem be more to anticipate from a former politician or wordsmith than what I could hope for from someone who dug up rocks for a living.

"Well he sure has a following, that's a huge crowd over there."

"What have we been talking about for the past couple of months? More people consuming more things. It's time we start putting this stuff together in a thought process that weaves the relevance and importance of that macro theme into opportunities."

"My pencil is sharp and notepad open. All we need now is a fresh cup of coffee and front row center seats."

We worked our way into the speaker hall and even though we were ten minutes ahead of the conference introduction, there was barely a seat to be had.

"Holy smokes, this place is packed."

"If you want really good seats, you gotta get here early."

We found ourselves a decent vantage point, centered to one of the large projection screens. The conference organizer, a well-known writer and newsletter publisher, outlined the focus and theme for the next three days: "Global Growth, Yes or No?", then gave a colorful introduction to the mining tycoon that detailed his background and experience.

While listening to the introduction and the guy's rather dynamite CV, I thought to myself that some forward-thinking TV network should produce a reality show about him, his life was so wild I was getting dizzy just hearing about it. In the course of a week he could be working on Wall Street, then take a break to fly deep into the jungles of Africa, then off to a movie premiere in Paris, in between which he would find time to share a scotch with any number of world leaders, all from the comfort of his own private jet.

Before I heard one word come from his mouth I had been captivated by the way he was described, which likened him to one of the iconoclasts that would be hanging out in the Argentine Galt's Gulch. The most incredible part of his legend was the unreal fact that the salary he took to run his entire empire was just one dollar per year. He only made money when his stakeholders made money. He was beyond a 4 percenter, he was a blend of Rockefeller, Steve Jobs and Teddy Roosevelt all wrapped up in one, and it was immediately clear I wanted to follow his economic soap opera.

But the question on every investor's mind sitting before him was "when will things be back to business as usual?" In the years following the 2008 economic collapse various economies had fluttered between marginal growth and a new word entered into the American lexicon that was old hat in the land of the rising sun – stagflation.

It was on everyone's lips, but nobody could answer that question nor could we expect our globetrotting mining executive to answer it for us. What we did receive was a tour de force on the nature of our changing world that began with a very memorable figure of speech.

"Before I begin I want you all to close your eyes and imagine you are a passenger riding on a train, rolling across the landscape. As a participant on this journey you have two choices: to sit facing the oncoming scenery or to place yourself on the flip side looking back on all that has passed. I'll give you a moment to decide."

Being a student of history, I chose to look back, and the landscape I imagined was much like the drive I took with Johnny through the Washington countryside. Skyscrapers blended into suburban communities, condos into factories, the oil refinery rushed past, and then came waves of evergreen trees and farmland.

"Investors with inadequate knowledge of history are frequently the most bearish. Let us use the past as a beacon to the future so we can all be a little less biased amongst a world filled with so much negativity. If you've chosen to sit looking forward you are able to see what may come ahead but you may have already forgotten how we arrived here. For those that chose the back facing view, you will be more prepared to build a comprehensive understanding of the future as you observe the changing landscape that forms the coming mountains and valleys. Both are good choices, however, for these uncertain times we want to look to the past to offer us clues as to what may happen as we forge ahead as a society."

It was a simply brilliant way to capture the attention and imagination of the listener, and it was the perfect set up for the gist of his presentation. To my delight, he continued with a series of historical examples to build up to his greater points about investing.

He noted there had only been two major changes at the number one spot in global economic rankings since the industrial revolution began. Britain, protected by the world's largest navy at the time and fuelled by world-leading reserves of coal and in turn, steel production, would overtake China and India at the onset of her industrial revolution.

In the fifty years following the American Civil War, the United States would overtake Britain as the world's largest economy and has held that position ever since. As he finished the arc to this point he stated that it would only be a matter of time until China, with the world's largest population, would reclaim the title she held for almost 2,000 years.

"What is surprising most of the decorated prognosticators at this time," he said. "Is the acceleration of when China should surpass the United States as the world's largest economy."

He went on to describe that in 1992 the gross domestic product of the United States was over $6 trillion while in China it was under $500 billion. Twenty years later the two countries' GDPs had climbed to $15 trillion and $9 trillion respectively. Who's catching up to who? In 1979 the average American was twenty times richer than the average Chinese citizen; now we were less than five times richer, and falling, as told by every economic gap closing these past decades.

Then he stated that one billion people in China still do not live like you and me. The first thought that came to my mind was Johnny's catch phrase about how no army, no government or no spiritual force could prevent that other one billion from participating in basic progress.

"If you have not been there, like many of the Sino-bears living out there in the financial permafrost then how can you know?"

It was true that many of the nattering naysayers had not been around the world. It had always been something that irked me. I'd rather draw my opinions from facts rather than assumptions.

"From up there, one can see what is down here," was a line that he clearly wanted to stick in everyone's mind as an image of hot air balloons floating over green fields filled the projection screen. He reiterated the fact that some of the deepest negativity, with respect to Asia and the growth bubbles people talked about, came from people who had never been there.

"I have been visiting Asia for thirty years and I have seen, first hand, the explosive growth. It is not that the American experience is over, far from it, but what is happening is the penthouse of power and influence around the world is getting bigger."

The idea of cultural differences was reinforced with the example how we in the west renovate whereas those in the east build anew. This was further established by highlighting the positive outlook that billions of people around the world still had. These folks were speculators to a more prosperous future and a speculator, by definition, was an optimist and not a pessimist, like so many beaten-down citizens in the west. I had to ask myself, where was global growth going to come from? The USA and Europe? Or from the hundreds of millions of emerging consumers?

"The biggest difference between the developed west and the emerging east is that when you multiply any number, no matter how small, by 2.5 billion, it becomes a very large number. In the west we used to have the capital and the know-how, now they have the capital, and they already know how. When it comes to leadership between the two there is a profound difference because most of the top political posts in China are held by people from the STEM fields. The members of the audience looking forward on our imaginary train probably forget what that stands for." he said with a cheeky grin and light laugh pointing at shadow figures.

"Let me refresh you, Science, Technology, Engineering and Math, the STEM fields are the very foundations of any nation's brainpower. What is the typical professional background of the average American politician? Lawyer. Imagine, the vast majority of our elected decision makers learn how to argue for a living. Is it any wonder little gets done in Congress, while the leaders of emerging economies learn how to build things?"

It was such a simple statement, yet the sobering reality of our country being led by lawyers gives one pause to think. In high school debate class, the seeds of interest for many lawyers, you are taught to argue both sides of a topic. When you have debated the topic to exhaustion they will flip your point of view and make you argue the other side of that position. These professional arguers are the people who are guiding our nation forward. If it wasn't so sad it might actually be funny.

"When it comes to public policy debates and infrastructure projects, we have limited representation by people who know how to make things. In China, they put their best and brightest at the helm, and it shows with their world-leading engineering and infrastructure projects. He elaborated on real GDP and the reliability of reported statistics. He noted the Chinese leadership has three key metrics they use to follow the strength of their economy – rail freight traffic, electricity consumption and debt and loan levels. "Are these not the pulse to the health of any economy?" he asked every person in the room.

"Where do you think the innovations of the future will come from?" he continued. "The choices made at the leadership level in any economy reverberate through the entire populace. In Western Europe it is easier to divorce your wife than it is to fire an employee. Where can there be greater innovation or optimism? In that atmosphere of seniority and entitlement, or in a place with far less business bureaucracy?"

It was true, in the west, one could obtain a divorce far easier that it was to adjust productivity in big industry. But this may be changing as hard-working young people around the world prefer the opportunity of a career to the stifling effects of impossible hiring conditions.

"A final thought about cultural differences is that the majority of products purchased in China are paid for in cash. These folks are not carrying monstrous amounts of credit card debts nor did they likely know, or care, that

Lehman Brothers collapsed during the economic crisis. Little has been able to derail the individual ambitions of these industrious new consumers."

We learned about CHINDIA and the BRIC countries with other examples of how cultural stereotypes were being torn down. India, a country with thousands of elaborately stratified social and hereditary hierarchies, is well known for its caste system. Now, in the new global economy, a young entrepreneur in the lowest caste can be the wealthiest guy in the village. I thought to myself what that would do to unleash human potential in the country with the second largest population in the world and a middle class larger than the United States.

"Since the financial economic crisis in 2008 there have been recessions all over the planet. Have there been many depressions? Has hyperinflation become rampant?"

He reiterated what Johnny had said about the differences between recessions and hyperinflation. Now I knew where he had picked up the jewel of information.

"It is imperative that every investor in this room understand that recessions rob people of what they might have as businesses and government curtail spending to an unknown future, but they do pass. Hyperinflation, on the other hand, robs people of what they already have. Thank goodness it has been eradicated from the developing world affording so many billions the confidence to strive for so much more."

There was simple common-sense factor to those two scenarios. A recession was a condition that we in the United States had faced many times in my lifetime. They were always terrible for the economy and almost every time they weighed heavy on my friends and family. But recessions do pass and confidence is rebuilt.

Hyperinflation was something that most people my age, particularly in the west, have never experienced. We have forgotten what that word really means and he reminded us all. When someone is no longer concerned about losing what they already have it surely unleashes the maximum in human potential. Hundreds of millions of people in countries around the world can celebrate that, as they too are not worried about the albatross of hyperinflation.

His presentation shifted gears into a series of stories supported by usable facts, and facts supported by memorable stories. He would coin a term and then spin a yarn that would go around the world and come back to end with everyone in the audience feeling like a sudden expert on that brand new term. One of these terms that would become the core statement of the entire trip was 'Airpocolypse.'

The developing world was becoming measurably wealthier, and that was a good thing. But their problem, and every human being's concern and opportunity, was an unprecedented level of smog choking the large cities of the Tiger economies. In the past, the citizenry would be left to suffer; but the time had come to finally deal with the environmental side effects of over thirty years of near 10% year-over-year growth.

China now had 300 million people with driver's licenses, and as I had learned from Johnny's lessons, it was, and shall remain, the largest automobile market in the world. Over twenty million new cars are sold in China every year, and one of the unfortunate byproducts of this stunning development were prolonged and heavy bouts of air pollution that plagued the citizens of her megacities. Asking these people to ditch their newly-purchased cars and walk to work was not realistic, but what would help this growing crisis was by making their emissions cleaner. And therein lay a very big opportunity that our keynoter was happy to explain to us.

"The way science makes gasoline and diesel engines cleaner is by capturing some of the tail pipe pollutants in a wondrous invention we call the catalytic converter. Palladium must be used for gasoline engines and platinum makes a diesel engine less pollutant, and these are things anyone for cleaner air can applaud," he went on to solve the concern and opportunity question. "Electric cars, which create zero emissions, need to be manufactured, fed and properly nourished. All three of these processes demand copper, way more copper. Hydrogen fuel cells, being embraced all over the world, need ounces of platinum, not tenths of ounces! Ladies and gentlemen, copper, palladium and platinum are your family of green metals, so if you are environmentally aware you'll want to become more familiar with them because they are the only things that help clean up the Airpocolypse."

This point struck an interesting chord within me. I'd always been a huge booster for the environment and alternative energy but never really acted on it. And I had definitely never drawn any parallel between the 'stuff' down there, and valuable green innovation up here. But why wasn't every investor piling into the inevitable theme of cleaner air in the developing world?

"How do they make electricity in China?" he questioned the crowd. "Coal, dirty brown coal, but that can't keep going on forever. Since Fukushima, Japan has turned off its nuclear reactors, so, now, how do they produce electricity? Coal and natural gas. Germany? They are trying one of the biggest green energy renaissances and copper thanks them for it. But for now, their base load power comes from guess what? Dirty brown coal. But the real question is how will they make electricity in the future? Green energy or any form of energy for that matter, requires one thing every time – copper."

He implored the crowd to never forget one fact that was undeniable no matter how many negative headlines they saw, "Power consumption has never done anything but gone up, and power needs copper." I heard it before from Johnny and now again from this experienced investor. This fact had now become biblical in nature.

"The Airpocolypse taking place in China's hundreds of cities, and all over the world, can only be cleaned up using more palladium, platinum and copper. And there is only one way they are able to secure it – by importing it from people like me who actually own it."

The most shocking new development he outlined was that copper's usefulness could potentially expand beyond many of today's standard applications. Hospitals had started using copper for countertops, door handles and other surfaces where bacteria were a problem.

"God forbid you should have to visit a hospital, but if you do please be aware of your surroundings. You are going to see more and more copper, the most natural surface to repel bacteria. Stainless steel is a magnet for the nasties that make people sicker when they leave the hospital than when they arrived."

He finished this thought by urging everyone to do their own research on the historic relevance of copper in the medical field. It had been a known antibody for keeping sickness at bay for millennia. The implications for copper were mind-blowing over and above all the other uses. As a doctor, I knew he was right, it was becoming more prevalent and when one multiplied the number of medical clinics across only the United States the implications for the copper industry were staggering.

"But things are serious and we continue to live in nervous times," he repeated this line twice. "If you invested in global growth ten years ago should you abandon that philosophy lock, stock and barrel due to potential stagflation in Europe and the West? Will the folks I just talked about stop being optimistic? Stop Growing? Stop consuming? Will the ghost cities you read about derail the migration of one billion people? Have governments in established economies done anything to repair their pathetic balance sheets? You all know the obvious answers to these simple but important questions," he stated. "Trillions of dollars have been printed and fed like drugs to greedy bankers while they secretly destroy your real spending power. How does one protect oneself? Own hard assets to retain real spending power! In China and other parts of the world copper is money, real money. Gold is money. Hard assets are money, they protect everyone's real spending power."

The allocated hour had passed so smoothly it was as if he had been telling one continuous story and nobody wanted it to end. It was a full hour of current events, an encyclopedia of data points and a least a half dozen unforgettable parables that everyone in attendance would recount for years to come.

All the while, this man who had made three fortunes in the world of mining, only whispered one sentence in support of his own prolific "green metal" deposits. The world could not live without his "green metals" and when they needed them, they would have to buy them from people like him. All he had to do was wait. I now had a thirst that needed to be quenched, and that thirst was the actual business and passion of this geology promoter. A 4 percenter who had shot way ahead to the front of the line of who I wanted to follow as my main economic soap opera.

"There has been lots of talk about the 1%, as everyone here can recall the backlash to the fat cats on Wall Street. Let me tell you, that is not the real 1%. Everyone here who is investing their valuable time and resources is in the true 1% and here's why. Ask any ten people outside of this very special atmosphere these simple questions and I guarantee you nine out of ten will get the answers wrong. In what measure do we value gold, iron ore, copper, wheat and beef and what is their current value? Knowing the answers to those questions, ladies and gentlemen, is your overwhelming advantage over 99% of the population, thus you are all in the real 1%."

The clever way he ended his talk reminded me of something Johnny said during our first meeting at my house. Whereas Johnny had used the example of a Big Mac, it now made far more sense to me knowing how much the 'stuff' that made a Big Mac possible actually cost. If a Big Mac was indexed to real inflation then it made absolutely no sense that government CPI, consumer price index, excluded fuel and food.

Truth be told, before I met Johnny I would have had no idea how much any of the building blocks to an economy were priced, let alone cost. There was great satisfaction knowing I too, was in the 1%.

9

Lunch With The Green Metal Maven

"If I hadn't been reading that newsletter you recommended I would have failed that quiz across the board," I said to Johnny as we walked out of the speaker hall.

"You get the point then?"

"Gold in ounces, copper in pounds, oil by the barrel, wheat in a bushel and cattle by the head."

"And more importantly you are current on the prices, so like in a soap opera, you can follow the daily, monthly, and yearly swings and you know how much all that 'stuff' actually costs."

As we filed into the showroom floor, Johnny guided me toward the exit door, and away from the maze of exhibiting investment opportunities.

"Where are we going?" I asked.

"To meet a friend, someone I think who can really explain the relevance of where all this 'stuff' comes from."

The hotel lobby was as busy as the conference itself, and hidden away in the middle of it all was none other than our billionaire mining tycoon chatting away into an ear piece and making a series of hand gestures. What was Johnny doing? Can we just go up to this guy and ask him questions? To my surprise he immediately ended his conversation as we approached.

"Gotta go," he said to whomever was on the other end, before turning and looking straight at Johnny.

"It's been a while, Sparky."

"A year to the minute."

I was dumbfounded at how Johnny was so cordially greeted by this man who had just received a standing ovation from a room full of sophisticated investors. Even more impressive was that it seemed quite clear that the meeting we were about to have had been planned well in advance.

"Who's your friend, another conversion?" The tycoon asked, extending his hand for a firm handshake.

"Doc Anderson, my family doctor; he's taken it upon himself to broaden his horizons about the world we live in."

"Welcome aboard Doc, were you able to pass my quiz at the end?"

"The answers were easy, now that I follow these kinds of things, but as Sparky here would tell you, I'm still working on the broader puzzle," I said.

"No need to bend your brain too much Doc, it's dead simple. People at large are rather oblivious to what's going on around them. They listen to the noise but they can't here the music."

"Follow me guys," Johnny said, as a crowd slowly began to build up around the perimeter of our conversation.

We walked out of the hotel, across the street and ducked into an alley to find a trendy little coffee shop. Johnny recounted how they first met at a conference in Munich, Germany and the life changing experience he had after hearing his first major keynote. The tycoon jokingly saw it a little differently, describing more than two years of relentless e-mails that "Sparky" had sent him before they finally crossed paths again.

"It was going to be pretty hard to get rid of someone that tenacious. I use to laugh to myself about whether or not this guy actually thinks I'm reading all the e-mails he was sending me."

"I started off asking you every question I could think of," Johnny explained. "And then I just went ahead and started sending you my blog every month."

"Wait, what blog?" I asked, genuinely surprised.

"So after a couple of years one of my bankers in Hong Kong forwards me this piece written by none other than Sparky here," said the Tycoon, apparently not hearing me. "I was bored on a flight so I read it, and it was good, damn good. I took note of it and the next time he mailed me I finally gave him a response."

"Ya, a two-word answer if I recall – 'nice work'." Johnny added.

"What was the blog about?" I asked.

Instead of answering my question, the maven nudged a middle-aged man standing in front of us in the coffee line.

"Excuse me, Sir, I have a little side bet with my friends and if you could answer this question I have to buy a round of coffees for everyone in the line."

"Hey friend, what you got? I'll do my best to get 'er right."

"How much does copper cost?"

"What?"

"Copper, the red metal."

"Like in a copper pipe? I don't have a dang clue. You got a question I might actually have a chance to answer?"

"Thanks pal, sorry to bother you, coffee's on me."

"Well, thank you very much."

"See what just happened there, Doc?"

"How do you expect him to answer that?" I asked, easing into being more comfortable with the first billionaire I'd ever met. He came off as sarcastic, so my gut feeling was to go with that tone in our chatter.

"Sparky's blogs were about exactly that. Very few people – and I'm talking even sophisticated folks – have the slightest clue where everything comes from, let alone the real price or value of it. The investment world has been polarized ever since the commodity prices took off in the early 2000's. Some analysts and investors think China is a bubble and when it explodes commodities will crash to their long-term averages, while others, me included, feel the growth phase around the world has a decade or two to run. Johnny's blog looks at both sides of the argument with the most important part being that the average guy walking down the street has no idea if commodities are fair value or overvalued."

As we sat down to drink our coffees, Johnny, or as we now called him, "Sparky," just leaned back and let the dialogue flow. It was clear that he was letting me enjoy the experience, while at the same time he could get his annual update from someone he truly admired. It was a great moment, and I was proud to be associated with Johnny, and appreciated how far he had gone out of his way to open up this entirely new world to me.

"Alright, first I want to let you know that I thought your presentation was brilliant, so let's just get that out of the way," I said. "Now, I don't want sound like a crabapple but

I have always considered myself to be an environmentalist, and it's no secret that your entire industry gets painted with a similarly caustic brush even though I can appreciate that there are good mines and bad mines. But how can I reconcile my beliefs with the possibility of investing in a mining operation?"

"Oh, you think you're an enviro-crusader?" He interrupted. "I am the world's biggest proponent of green energy, and, in turn, I'm a realistic environmentalist. I imagine a world where year after year we support and explore new technologies that make the possibility of burning less fossil fuels possible. That's the environmentalist part. I'm realistic because if we want to burn less coal, natural gas- and oil, all of which are finite resources, we have no choice but to have reliable access to the building blocks that make these long-term solutions possible for the generations to come. Now here's a question for you – will there be more or less electric automobiles in the coming decades?"

"Well, the problem with electric cars is range and reliability, but yes I think anyone could agree we'll see more brands adopting electric models and consumers will likely buy more."

"Great, now how are we going to charge these cars?"

"With electricity, of course."

"What kind of electricity? What most people forget is that we still need to fuel these cars with power, electric power, and most of the world's electricity comes from oil, gas and coal. I vote for less fossil-fuel electricity and more innovation, more green energy and more people making it possible."

"Ok, so as Sparky would tell us, the greener and cleaner we create energy, the more that is demanded of copper."

"Yes, society needs to have access to copper, it's not just the red metal, it's also the green metal. There is little wonder it oxidizes into a brilliant turquoise green, perhaps the big man upstairs was giving mankind a clue as to its many magical uses."

"Point taken, but it's going to take a little more convincing before I become a raving promoter of hard rock mining."

"Let's assume you are the biggest environmentalist in the world. We can both agree that it is very inefficient dictating policy to people in the developing world, correct?"

"We can use awareness and innovation; nobody wants to breathe polluted air. However, demanding that people in growing parts of the world install deluxe systems to capture carbon has proven to be a very difficult discussion. That much we can agree on."

"So perhaps a better way is to inform and educate. At a minimum even hardened greenies needs to fly to their meetings, or ride a bicycle to get around, take hot showers and watch engaging programs to stay current. Do they make bamboo airplanes? Can they print books without paper? Or can you read the latest Greenpeace missive on your e-reader without plugging it into a wall? How can they deliver the seeds for your community garden and where is the water coming from to make it grow? Where do you think the building blocks to every single thing you are looking at come from? The earth, that's where."

"Johnny and I have already had this discussion," I replied. "All the stuff from up here, most of which now has an electrical cord sticking out the back of it, comes from the commodities down there."

"Precisely. Glad we agree on that. The second part of it is to acknowledge that we, the west, or the green movement, cannot prevent them, the developing world, from having what you and I take for granted. They are not marching to the same tune that protesters are drumming; they simply want a better, healthier and more comfortable life for their families."

"There is no army, no government and no spiritual force that can stop them," I said.

"Hey! That's my line!" the billionaire snapped back.

Johnny busted in to give credit for his mantra to the tycoon. You could see how a decade of being a participant as a contrarian had rubbed off on him: It was already beginning to shape the verbs and nouns I was using.

"The other thing that we cannot control is the urbanization of these people. In the past twenty years, around 500 million people have been removed from poverty. The 500 million before them took a staggering 100 years because change took so much longer before. It is estimated that the next 500 million will begin to participate in some kind of city life in only one decade. Imagine the progress that has been created needs to double. Again!"

"So if mankind cannot stop this massive migration, isn't it everyone's duty to come up with better long-term solutions that help these new consumers and everyone else?"

"That's true, we can't stop them. So, as an investor you have two choices – to become a victim or to become a contrarian, or as I prefer to say a participant. You have probably heard the term NIMBY right?" the tycoon asked me pointedly.

"Not in my backyard."

"Now there's even a more extreme version of that phenomenon called 'BANANA' - build-absolutely-nothing-anywhere-near-anyone. This is great if you don't need things like bikes, hospitals or food – things that tend to come in quite handy in New York City, Tokyo or even Bangladesh. Yet there is a group of people who want zero development and zero progress for everyone else while they already live in a world with all the comforts entitled to them. I think I once read Einstein as saying something like 'it's easier to split an atom than it is to change a pre-determined opinion.' A better position, in my own personal opinion of course, is to extract the things the human race cannot live without in the absolute best way possible."

"So that's what makes you the world's pre-eminent environmentalist? You want to mine those things that promote a greener world and you want to do it in the cleanest, safest way possible?"

"Absolutely, but let's go one step further – can we also agree that you and I as environmentally conscious people will be very ineffective in dictating terms to government and industry in China, India and the rest of the developing world?"

"Yes, of course, they would be harder to convince, and even some Western governments. We can all remember what happened to the Kyoto Protocol."

"Can we also agree that the human race needs 'stuff', and advocating the BANANA brand of progress is unrealistic and quite literally impossible?"

"Again, I can't argue with that line of thinking."

"And can we finally agree that responsible mineral extraction is what my industry's brainpower and bandwidth should be focusing on in order to promote and provide the products that enhance a greener world?"

"You're on a roll now, and if it's done properly I would assume it should benefit all the stakeholders involved."

"Now that we're in agreement on the basic principle of mining, let's talk about the lifeblood of any economy. The undisputed king of metals, and the metal that must be used when societies and industry want cleaner power or clearer skies."

"Copper."

"Exactly. Copper, the truly green metal, it's just disguised in red."

"So you are also saying that, hypothetically, we could live without oil, or let's say far less oil, coal and other fossil fuels if we substituted more copper?"

"Sparky, this is going to be Doc Anderson's lucky day."

"How so?" Asked Johnny, who had remained silent while the tycoon and I had argued over our environmental credentials.

"You're from the Pacific Northwest, so naturally you're a greenie, you guys are the pioneers of the movement," the tycoon continued.

"So why is it my lucky day?" I asked.

"Because you've positively nailed it. Think about the implications of your statement. Can our society, or any other one for that matter, use far less fossil fuels? The answer we all now know is a resounding yes. What makes it possible? By going greener and cleaner. Among other things, copper is the cornerstone of this strategy. Today, tomorrow and far into the future."

"Ok, but I'm still missing how knowing this makes today my lucky day."

"I have an hour before my first official meeting. Plus, I missed breakfast so I'm going to grab an early lunch. Due to Sparky's tutelage, you now know where copper was used, is used, and most importantly, will be used in increasing quantities due to the line you like to use, everything we buy comes with an electrical cord sticking out the back. So what we are going to do in the next hour is make you an expert on where copper came from, comes from, and for the purpose of your lucky day, where future resources of copper will come from. Let's call it the Cole's Notes version of copper mining 101."

"I'm going to learn all of this over lunch?"

"I said the Cole's Notes version, Doc, and typically you need to be one very large investor to get this attention."

"Oh, I'm not complaining."

As we left the coffee shop and walked a couple of blocks to a nearby steak house, we reestablished the foundation of the Copper Mining 101 lesson: Firstly, global electricity consumption has done nothing in the past 100 years but go up. No copper meant no electricity, period. Secondly, we agreed, as environmentally conscious individuals, that we do need responsible natural resource development, and it is the industry's responsibility to provide reliable access to resources so the world can adopt greener solutions.

When we took our seats for lunch, the tycoon requested that both Johnny and I sit across from him. It still seemed odd to me that someone as prolific as he was would take the time to sit down with us. Johnny was right all along, this was a unique industry. It would be impossible to achieve an even remotely similar level of access to a hi-tech billionaire.

"Don't get me wrong when I ask this, because I am humbled you would take the time to explain your philosophy to me, but why exactly are you having lunch with a lowly middle-aged family doctor?"

"Oh that part, I guess Sparky didn't tell you. You only have one minor responsibility once you have finished your Copper Mining 101 course."

"Here we go. Let me guess, I have to buy your stock?"

"Ha! No, you're not going to move the needle for me if you do that, but you do need to become a proactive environmentalist and that means you have to promise to be an ambassador of the green metal."

"I'm already sold on that, I just hope I can keep up with what you put down!"

"The most important principle for your copper mining education is to know the difference between supply and demand. Demand, as you already know, is anything that has copper in it while supply means mining new material and recycling old products. Demand for copper has grown by over 3% per year since 1900 and during some periods as high as 5%. I would suggest that this 3% growth is a very reliable statistic. Let's call it a constant."

"And if we apply the rule of 72 we then know that global demand for copper has doubled approximately every 24 years or so."

"Very good, this will be easy for you but demand isn't the issue, the question is, whether or not supply can keep up."

"Come again?"

"Too much copper being supplied against reliable demand should equal low prices while too little copper being supplied should create a premium."

"I thought you said mining 101, seems to me you just described economics 101 – the laws of supply and demand."

"I like to use the analogy of musical chairs to explain just that, supply and demand. If there are 99 people trying to sit in 100 chairs could there ever be a premium for chairs? Obviously not. But what happens if all of sudden there are 101 or 102 people trying to sit in 100 chairs? Voila! Who knows what someone will pay to have a chair when that happens. Over the past forty years copper has been supplied, mainly from old legacy mines, and has more or less lagged or kept up with demand. Which we recall has been very reliable, growing between 3% and 5%. So to be crystal clear, for most of the past forty years there has almost always been just a bit too much, or at times, far too much copper supply available."

"Which makes a premium next to impossible."

"You're acing the test. So let's define what supply really means in this instance. Copper ore, classified as a rock that has a mineral resource in it, is mined, usually blasted with explosives in a large open pit or underground, and then transported to be processed. Processing takes place one of two ways; the conventional way called flotation or a more modern way called solvent extraction. I'll explain both real quickly. Flotation was developed in the early days of modern mining and has been the most widely used method since. In the late 1960s a new type of processing was developed called solvent extraction and electrowinning, often called S-X-E-W."

"This is getting pretty deep; you're starting to lose me with all the jargon."

"Relax, this sets up the reason copper prices were low for forty years. The basic difference between the two types of processing, for your understanding, is that flotation concentrates copper ore so that it can be economically shipped for final smelting and refinement. Copper ore in the ground, on global average scale, is now less than 1% copper and over 99% waste rock. That means it needs to be bumped up, or concentrated to have 25% to 40% copper content. Then this super high-grade material is sent for smelting, a term you have likely heard before?"

"That's where they melt the metal down to become pure copper, right?"

"Exactly. Smelting takes this concentrated material to 99%, at which point it is refined to pure copper form – which is the red metal that you see in copper cable or piping."

"Ok so what about SXEW? What's the difference?"

"Solvent extraction is a two-stage hydrometallurgical process that was developed, optimized, and put into large-scale use in the United States during the '80s and Chile during the '90s. This was important as it was able to monetize very low-grade copper ore, often found in waste dumps at major mines, which were previously uneconomic. This process occurs entirely at the mine site as the SX portion extracts leachable copper and then is processed by electrowinning – the EW part – into 99% copper metal. When this copper leaves the mine site it is ready for final refinement to pure copper so there is no smelting needed."

"You weren't joking when you said this would be copper 101. So how does this affect supply and demand?"

"You already know that copper is sold in pounds, however, on the large international metals exchanges, where excess copper supply goes, it is sold in tonnes, a tonne being approximately 2,200 pounds. Imagine that for forty years, from the '60s to the early 2000s, copper prices fluctuated in dimes ranging from 60 cents per pound to just over a dollar."

"Is that why many analysts and pundits feel copper prices should correct to the levels of a reliable forty year price cycle?"

"Remember the musical chair analogy? For those forty years there was almost always a little too much metal supply. There were a few reasons for that. First of all, the big mining companies were run by men who measured their egos by building bigger and bigger mines. The biggest mines in the world today were not built in the recent cycle. Another major reason was the number of end-use customers declined. After World War Two, the west became developed to the point that the per-person consumption of copper and other metals stagnated just as all this 'new' supply kept coming on stream. Then through the '80s and '90s, new technologies like SXEW exacerbated the oversupply. Finally, just when the world was absolutely awash in copper, the Cold War ended and another wave of 'cheap' throwaway metal hit the market. When the Berlin Wall fell on November 9, 1989, the Iron Curtain opened further copper supplies from three of the largest mining complexes in the world. They stopped feeding the military machine and dumped all that metal into an already over-supplied market."

"So for all those years we had too many chairs and not enough people to sit in them?" I asked.

"The price of copper in 2002 hit an absolute all-time inflation adjusted low of less than 70 cents per pound, lower than it was for the most of the '70s and '80's."

"So what changed?"

"The industry finally stopped building new copper mines. They didn't stop there though; through the '90s most of the big mining companies curtailed spending and laid off their exploration teams who are like the research-and-development divisions of natural resource companies. Where was future supply going to come from? If nobody is constructing new supply what happens in the future? We remember even in the lean years demand always grew, all the while new customers finally did enter the market and they were growing their economies by 10% per year. Unlike developed countries, these folks were starting from a very low base so they needed the basic building blocks of nationhood. They needed the copper, steel and oil to grow, kind of like the United States and Europe at the turn of the last century."

"Let me digest this. The price of copper in 2002 was 70 cents per pound, the same as it was for a large part of the '70s and '80s. How much profit was there for the copper mining industry?"

"Profit? In 2002? You must be joking. A stockbroker friend of mine had a great line for that situation about how mining companies could make up their losses by increasing volume! Mining was the laughing stock of the investment world, a perfect page sixteen story. Years of continued growth in emerging markets slowly but surely absorbed the idiotic oversupply of copper metal, a three-decade-long hangover. In October 2003, the tipping point occurred. What the market forgot was that supply could be disrupted by numerous unforeseen circumstances like power outages, strikes or weather."

"So you're saying that the demand is reliable, and you have the statistics to prove it, but supply turns off in a blink when something happens."

"Does it ever. The most serious type of supply disruption is an act of God, and boy did the copper mining industry get one in October of 2003, that acted as the tipping point that ended decades of really low prices. Grasberg, the world's second largest copper mine in Indonesia was shut down instantly after a massive pit wall collapse."

"Pit wall collapse?"

"Yes, due to way too much rain, the entire side wall of that humongous open pit collapsed and the mine would be shut down for an undetermined period of time. The fallout was that everyone who followed, produced, or purchased copper, scrambled to cover the massive copper supply deficit that would surely follow. This one copper mine supplied 5% of the world's copper at the time."

"So that caused the musical chairs to become a premium and the price of copper finally jumped from those absurd lows?"

"You bet! That tipping point drove the price of copper from 70 cents per pound to $4.00 per pound in early 2006, an unprecedented jump. Remember the price of copper used to fluctuate in dimes and then suddenly it jumped over $3.00 per pound in two and half years."

"What a business!"

"The problem was that nobody in the industry could believe it either. Most of the executives, professionals and participants in the copper mining industry thought it was unsustainable. Many of them cashed in their stock options as the price of copper inched its way up, never dreaming it could ever sustain itself past $1.00 per pound."

"These companies making copper must have started to make profits hand over fist if they were used to selling it for 70 or 80 cents and could now sell for $3.00 per pound or more?"

"Some companies prospered but some recognizable copper miners hedged their futures down the toilet. In their wisdom, the same 'insiders' who cashed in their stock options when copper climbed over a dollar were hedging future production at that idiotic 85 cents level and even further as prices reached $1.25. There is a great maxim coined by a Chicago-based economic historian to describe this. He stated: 'Invest in an industry where those that know it best, love it least, because they've been disappointed most.'"

"Ouch, so they locked in the sale of their future supply at 85 cents and $1.25 while prices climbed to over $3.00 per pound? What happened to those companies?"

"Take a guess. All of their choice assets were gobbled up on the cheap by competitors. They knew the copper mining industry as well as anyone else, and they had been punished for decades by low copper prices so they had no confidence, if only they better understood they had hundreds of millions of new customers."

"The new spending class became the new customers of Big Copper."

"The famous investor, Sir John Templeton would cringe if he heard someone go against his 'it's different this time' quote, which he said were the four most dangerous words in investing, but this time it WAS different. Those hundreds of millions of people were urbanizing, and the copper mining executives failed to see that."

"So is this still confusing the market? If those executives, who were supposed to be the 'experts' in copper mining, could miss such an obvious change taking place in the world, could the same thing be happening now?"

"I've already told you that the so-called experts who follow copper mining, and commodities in general, have never been so polarized," the maven continued. "Seeing is believing, and it will take you a lot more research to become truly familiar. But the one thing that we do know with a high degree of confidence is that one billion new consumers will demand access to basic progress in the next ten to twenty years."

"The answer comes in the reliable concept that these people will continue to consume more things – which I think is unstoppable."

"But to get back on topic, where does all this copper come from, which countries and how many mines are we talking about?"

He let that question linger for a few moments while we pondered it. Then he began again.

"The days are over when big mining companies could choose where to invest. Anyone who thought or still thinks that politics are not relevant to commodity prices, or where and how one engages in extractive industries, is either a fool or a damn fool. The biggest producer of copper is Chile and the biggest consumer of copper is China -- those are the facts. Primary copper production comes from mining, thus the word 'primary,' and secondary production comes from recycling, which is around 15% of the market."

"So you're telling us that the existing mines, these so called legacy mines, are located in established places? So how many mines are we talking about?"

"I'm getting to that in two seconds. We already know that demand has grown by over 3% per annum for over a century. The problem we now face is keeping supply up with the pace of demand. In 2012 the world used 20 million tonnes of copper for the first time. If demand growth is 3% that would suggest we need 600,000 tonnes of new copper production to keep up with reliable demand, not even factoring in mine closures and reserve depletion. You don't think these mines last forever, do you?"

"So how much is 600,000 tonnes? Is that a small, medium or large copper mine? And how many mines are we talking about to produce say 50% of the worlds new copper each year?"

"The top fifteen major mines account for about 50% of primary copper production, which is incredible if you stop and think about it. Only fifteen mines! The largest mine in the world, located in Chile, produced 1 million tonnes that same year in 2012. The bulk of the large mines in the top fifteen produce an average of 250,000 to 300,000 tonnes of copper metal per year. So, to answer your question the long way around, the industry needs to build two or three significant mines each year to keep up with the very reliable 3% growth rate. What about 4% or 5% growth like most of the past decade? Do you know how much a copper mine that can yield 250,000 tonnes a year costs to build?"

"No idea, I'm going to guess quite a bit."

"Modern mines of that size, with all the added costs associated with safety and environmental safeguards, cost $5 billion, or more, to build. Gone are the days of building infrastructure in a world with cheap $20-per-barrel oil. Twenty and thirty years ago $1 billion dollars went a long way to completing a major mine, today it's not even the down payment."

"Hold on. A minute ago you told me the days are over where big mining companies can choose where to invest; that means they are running out of "safe" and "easy" places to build new mines. You also told me that the research and development arms of most major mining companies were shut down during the decades of low copper prices. Now, you are saying we need to build three medium-sized mines each year just to keep up with demand. And it costs three or four times more for each tonne of production? How are they doing this?"

"They aren't, and that is my *raison d'etre*. The longer period of time that no meaningful new production comes on-line, the more the coil is sprung for higher long-term copper prices. As well, the deposits of the future have been left to smaller companies that are focused on the R&D part of the business and less so on the development side. Also, they're often fielded by the very geologists and engineers the big companies fired in the '80s and 90s. People like me will sell our high quality mineral deposits to the major companies when they are ready to invest in development. But they need higher long-term prices – that's their insurance policy, and yours too."

"These are the speculative junior mining stocks that scare the pants off of people like me." I admitted.

"Sadly you are right. There is so much stupidity that enters otherwise rational thinking that the majority of small investors are often fleeced."

This was a sound time for Johnny to jump in with his memorable George Bernard Shaw quote: "It was created by the upper classes and the lower classes to fleece the middle classes."

"Who you follow for investments is your business," the maven continued. "My job here is to provide the foundation to answer the question – where is all this stuff going to come from? Here are the hard numbers. We keep talking about the decade between 2002 and 2012 because so much activity took place in natural resources when the metal prices skyrocketed. In 2002 - $2.2 billion of capital was raised for speculative exploration, R&D if you want to call it that, in natural resources companies. In 2012, the busiest year on record until that date, $29.2 billion was raised. In fact, between 2002 and 2012 $136 billion was raised worldwide on non-bulk commodity exploration. It has been reported that there were 647 significant new mineral discoveries in that time span. However, only 18 of them were considered to be top-tier. Even though there was a ten-fold increase in dollars toward R&D it simply did not yield a proportionate level of results."

"How can that be? I asked. "How does any industry spend ten times more money and come up with so little for it?"

"One of the reasons is due to so little expertise. Remember, the mining industry as a whole went through a dark ages when there was very little learning. Who wanted to become a geologist in the '90s? Everyone wanted to be a computer programmer, and entire geological departments were shut down at major universities. Many who did choose to become extractive industry professionals didn't go to work for mining companies, but rather went to work with non-governmental organizations that were trying to stop development."

"I can see that. But there must have been a more important reason there were disappointing results at finding future mineral deposits after a ten-fold increase in R&D money?"

"The sobering fact is that all the low hanging fruit has been picked."

"You are trying to tell me that mining is now an extremely difficult business, aren't you?"

"The days of building a mine from discovery to production in five years are long gone. On average it now takes fifteen years from discovery before a company can have the first pound of copper come out of the ground. Also, the grades are much lower than they were in the past.

You recall I said it was 1% copper and 99% waste rock? That was twenty and thirty years ago: now the average grade of a copper mine is 0.6% of copper and 99.4% waste rock, which means miners need to move, on average, almost twice as much rock for the same amount of metal yield they realized in the past."

"Wow, when you look at it that it way it makes a huge difference. That measly .4% of a difference in falling grade, means they have to mine almost twice as much rock! When you're talking about billions of tonnes it's a lot!"

"Modern deposits are going to be deeper, more remote and frequently in countries that don't have the same political surety as Arizona or Chile. Not only is it difficult and hard to find new deposits in remote parts of the world, imagine what it does to costs when you explore and develop, with no infrastructure, in less-friendly places? The distant future of copper mining will need to take place in countries like Mongolia, Pakistan, Congo and even Afghanistan. For the obvious reasons of safety and feasibility, there is no reassurance that some of those prolific deposits will ever be developed."

"If the industry is that difficult and riddled with so many challenges then why even bother?"

"Oh but that's the fantastic opportunity. If the world needs as much copper in the next twenty years as has been consumed in the past one hundred years, and that is the proportional scale, then where is it going to come from?"

I shuttered in the thought that I had a far better understanding than 99% of the investing public about this circumstance and opportunity.

"Perhaps in the high-quality deposits that have already been discovered?" he answered his own question. "A company holding unhedged copper reserves in a politically stable part of the world offers tremendous leverage to future copper pricing. And remember, because the copper is 'in the ground' there is no storage cost and as such it's being sold at pennies per pound in the ground. To make these reserves financially viable, there must be higher long-term copper prices. That is your insurance policy to higher future prices."

It made sense, but I couldn't help but think that if mining is a difficult business that makes it both an opportunity, due to the tremendous leverage being offered, and a hazard, which came from the many pitfalls involved. These, in turn, seemed to be more plentiful than in other sectors and could easily trip up an investor. However, the opportunity was fortified by the trend of reliable growth in population, electricity consumption and the largest migration of human beings in history. In the opinion of the 4 percenter I just had lunch with, the next great copper deposit to be developed has already been found and all investors like myself had to do was locate them and wait.

"So where will the price of copper go?" I asked the maven as we paid our bill. I pulled out my credit card, but he waved his hand and continued to orate.

"I have no idea, but as long as we have an atmosphere where 100 people are trying to sit in 99 chairs we should see 'stronger for longer' copper prices. The second part of the question is – will there be more or less uses for copper? The media can discuss this point until they are blue in the face but I am quite confident that there will be more people next year and in the next decade. I'm also confident that they will want more basic comforts and that they will have the ability to pay for them. It makes it very hard for me to follow anyone who has not really been to Asia and seen with their own eyes what is really going on."

"I've never been. Never really thought much about it until I met Sparky."

"I bet you don't even have a passport do you?"

"No, I don't. My wife, ex-wife I mean, and I used to go to Mexico, but that was years ago when we just needed to show our drivers license."

"Well you are not alone. The vast majority of Americans have never even applied for a passport. You now have a broader education than most people as to why commodities are so important to mankind. The single biggest piece of advice I am going to leave with you trumps everything else we've talked about."

I could hardly wait, this was the moment where he was going to hand me the holy grail. Did he do the same to Johnny all those years ago enabling him to find financial freedom in his 30's? Was he going to give me the hottest stock tip of the entire Conference?

"My advice to you is to go see the world, and start where it's really going to matter to your future, go to China."

"China?" I sighed.

10

Planes, Trains & Rickshaws

After returning home from the conference I immediately began the process to obtain my first passport. When I thought about it, it was silly: How could a well-off, 58 year-old American professional have never even applied for a passport? Being in the company of Johnny and other contrarians I felt more than a little embarrassed. In fact, I was downright angry with myself. What had I been missing all of these years?

All in all it took only two weeks for my passport to arrive based on my urgency to have it in hand and apply for a travel visa, so I could take my first overseas trip. Johnny had some business to do in China, and offered to go a little earlier so we could go on a fact-finding, cross-country road trip if I came along. So I jumped at the opportunity and bought a plane ticket.

The visa application part of our trip planning was surprisingly easy: There are numerous businesses that offer visa services and promise a turnover in only a few business days. The main driver for these visa centers weren't Yankees like me going to China, but the droves of mainland Chinese who were coming to North America, en masse, for tourism. Who would have thought that?

Our plan was to fly into Hong Kong, now a specially administrated zone within The People's Republic of China, and travel by train to our first destination of Guangzhou. This way we could also see Shenzhen, which lay between Hong Kong and Guangzhou. Later we would check out the granddaddy of all electrical generation projects, the Three Gorges Dam, then skip through Shanghai on our way to Beijing, finally ending our trip at the Great Wall of China.

A couple of days before the trip I had a panic attack and wanted to call the whole thing off when I started to contemplate the fourteen-hour flight. I asked myself what in bloody hell was I doing? Six months ago I was a divorcee fumbling around in the dark with a bag full of wires, convinced that the remainder of my days would end up being a predictable series of evenings spent falling asleep on the couch. And now I was shuttering my medical practice for two weeks and flying off to China to bear witness to "the single largest migration of human beings in the history of the world."

All the time I had spent with Johnny attending the conference, plus my countless hours of reading and research, had made me a believer, but I was not without skepticism. If I had one takeaway about the economies of emerging markets it's that there was always the calamitous threat of a massive market correction, or even worse, social upheaval looming over their development boom. Maybe it was just naysayer hoopla used to sell magazines, but I couldn't shake the image of a tumbleweed floating through a massive, unoccupied ghost city. If I'd learned one thing about investing, it was to stay away from bubbles. But that ran contrary to the concept of embracing volatility, the philosophical heart of contrarian investing.

I remembered once again to invest in the story on page sixteen that is on its way to page one. The problem was that China was all over the cover pages of global media – the real page sixteen story was commodities, energy consumption and how they would be affected by China. If I was going to really understand this convergence I would need to go see it myself, so I decided to throw caution to the wind and pack my bags for a painful fourteen hour flight in cabin class.

In the meanwhile, I took the maven's advice and looked deeper into some potential ways copper could serve other purposes. A number of notable studies had demonstrated that replacing surfaces and objects made with the red metal did indeed cut the risk of infection. As he put it, stainless steel was like a magnet for bacteria while copper was a repellant. It was only a matter of time before this became a standard throughout hospitals, or at least well-funded hospitals, all over the world. But that was a small slice of the global economy, so I started studying a sector I should have been following all along – green technology and clean energy.

When you dug a little deeper into green energy it became clear rather quickly that whether it was wind farms, solar panels, or electric vehicles, anything that was going to make this world greener and cleaner always revolved around electricity, and the common bond in every case was copper.

Green energy's relationship to the Chinese market was equally inextricable. In the case of solar power, over the past few years China grew to dominate the solar-cell market simply due to the sheer size of its manufacturing base. The issue of price had always dogged the marketability of these cells. But because China had gained a foothold in the market, and had the scale to produce in bulk with plentiful access to cheap production materials, voila, they had knocked the price down substantially. These lower prices would naturally make the technology far more appealing to consumers than reasons of pure environmental altruism.

Beyond China's ability to out-produce most other countries, what had made these new cells even more affordable? Copper, of course. By using copper instead of silver for the cell's electrical contact lines, Chinese manufacturers had cut production costs by over half in just a few years.

I'd made a few attempts to calculate how much copper would be needed just to feed the demand of green energy and the numbers left my head spinning. Every bit of research I did helped me gain more confidence and nuanced perspective. I began to understand more about what 'stuff' up here needed which 'stuff' down there. But I didn't want to limit myself to any one sector or technology. If I was going to invest, I wanted to invest in all of it, including both the supply and the demand and my Asian adventure was going to help out in spades.

When I got to the airport, Johnny was waiting for me at the Cathay Pacific counter as planned. As usual he was even more on the dot than me, self-proclaimed Mr. Punctual.

"Hey Doc, long time no see. Wow that's a big suitcase, did you bring all your tools?"

I looked at my suitcase, admittedly bulky, and compared it to the slick leather duffle bag Johnny had hanging from his shoulder and I threw my hands up in surrender.

"Johnny, we're going for ten days aren't we? I thought I'd at least bring a suit and a change of shoes."

"That's alright, we have time to adjust that. Now you're going to find out why they have luggage shops at the airport."

"And do what with this?" I said as I pointed to my jumbo sized suitcase.

Johnny seemed to have an answer for everything. In the span of twenty minutes we had purchased a sturdy yet compact carry-on trolley type suitcase. To my astonishment all the important items fit with room to spare. We then threw the behemoth into a storage locker and worked our way toward security. Clearly, it was going to be easier to navigate the planes, trains and rickshaws in this manner. I was relieved.

After we boarded and settled into our seats, I took out a list of points I wanted to reflect on during the flight. For all the things I had accomplished over the past months, this trip would be my final exam. I'd graduated from paying peanuts for monkeys to spending good money on a few quality newsletters, and as a result it felt like I'd gained ten or twenty investment IQ points.

Equipped with this heightened awareness, I'd begun to follow a number of different financial soap operas, and even identified a couple of my own 4 percenters for each of them. The foundation was firmly in place, and the only thing left to do as an investor was to officially make the switch from passive to active by moving some of my investment dollars into the speculative arena.

***

Luckily, I was able to catch some solid REM sleep on the plane, so as we touched down on the tarmac a full day after we left Sea-Tac, I was feeling somewhat refreshed. But maybe that was just the adrenaline of adventure entering my bloodstream.

Walking into the airport, I didn't know exactly what to expect. For whatever reason, call it ignorance, I thought it was going to be a dump. What I found was the newest and cleanest airport I'd ever stepped foot in. As we cleared customs at Hong Kong International, no visa required, Johnny described the sky-high real estate values in the area. And I thought Manhattan was expensive.

After a quick transfer in downtown Hong Kong we boarded a commuter train for Shenzhen where we would transfer to Guangzhou. On the way, Johnny gave me a brief history lesson on the region.

"Shenzhen is where it all started. It was China's first Special Economic Zone which gave it special economic policies and flexible government measures. In 1979 it was just a village and it is now one of the fastest growing cities in the world. Guangzhou on the other hand, formerly Canton, was the starting point of the Maritime Silk Road and was for centuries China's most important seaport. It's another city where China began its experiment with capitalism back in the '80s. This city used to be the center of the economic universe, and it's on its way to reclaiming that title."

"So when China had the largest GDP in the world for a couple thousand years, this place was pretty important wasn't it?"

"Sure was, and it is again. It's magnificent what has been built between Hong Kong and Guangzhou in the past three decades alone."

"So how far is our hotel from here, Johnny?"

"We'll be there in less than two hours and we're staying downtown, but when we get to the main station we're going to take a cab because there's something on the way I want to see."

"Hey, I thought this was a fact-finding mission and not some tourist trip."

"It's going to be a bit of both, but rest assured we're not going to be spending too much time mulling around old temples. If we're going to be touring anything it'll be the temples of the future."

A string of shiny new taxis was waiting for us outside Guangzhou's main train station, and to my surprise, most of them were some kind of weird Volkswagen hybrid.

"What, no rickshaws?" I quipped.

"Doc, you'd have a way better chance finding a rickshaw back home than you would in most cities in modern China. This city has a GDP of nearly two hundred and fifty billion dollars, that's more than San Francisco, which happens to be the rickshaw capital of the US."

Johnny opened the door of the first taxi in line and rattled off some rapid-fire Chinese. The driver looked back at us with a surprised expression but then shrugged and popped the trunk.

"So you do speak Mandarin?"

"I can speak taxi Cantonese or Mandarin, you kind of need both in these parts and it's going to help us get to where we're going."

"And where is that?"

"To a factory."

"And here I thought we were done with surprises. How foolish of me."

Soon after leaving the train station, we found ourselves on a busy ten-lane highway that had loops and overpasses unfurling in every direction. We sidestepped a massive traffic jam and took an off-ramp into an industrial zone where a ceaseless string of gigantic factories whizzed by in the rearview mirror, while mountains of high-rises dipped in and out of sight in the background. From what I could see, the city stretched on forever towards the horizon.

"I really should have checked this before we left, but how big is this city?"

"Greater Guangzhou has a population of around 40 million people, that includes its neighboring city of

Shenzhen of course – so double the New York/New Jersey metro area."

"Sweet Jesus that's a lot of people."

"You probably noticed there was no real stop to the urbanization from H.K. all the way here. A hundred miles without a break, it's breathtaking really."

After ten or so minutes, our cabbie pulled over to the shoulder and he and Johnny exchanged some more Mandarin before the driver gave another shrug.

"Here we are."

"Where is here?"

"Let's get out and I'll show you."

On the right hand side was a very large factory, and on the other side of the road was the construction footprint to what looked to be an even bigger one.

"This plant produces nearly half a million cars per year, that's more than America's busiest automobile factory. And you see that construction site over there? That will soon be another plant that will make even more cars on an annual basis. Right now every car company on the planet is clamouring to come here and build plants like this – Ford, Volkswagen, Fiat, GM, Toyota, everyone, because in almost every case it is now their largest market. They're all eager to spend billions here because the Chinese appetite to own an automobile is insatiable. Remember that timeline we talked about, how in 1979 there were just sixty-privately owned cars in China and now there are over two hundred and fifty million vehicles? Car ownership in China has exploded; in fact, between 2005 and 2010 it doubled! Now they make over 50,000 cars a day, that's up 1,000% in the past couple of decades. And still only a small portion of China's 1.35 billion people actually own a car. So do you think that this trend is going to come to a grinding halt?"

"Well, that depends on if their economy keeps on growing, doesn't it?"

"If the Chinese economy continues apace at 7% or 8% growth, China is expected to be making more cars than North America and Europe combined by the year 2020. And even then, 40% of the Chinese population will still live in rural areas. In the past three decades, since Deng Xiaoping launched their capitalist spirits, over three hundred million Chinese have left poverty to come to places like Guangzhou and Shenzhen. The vast majority of those people are just now buying their first car. The real question is how long will it take the next 100 million or 500 million people? And then how about the 2.5 billion people in CHINDIA who are going to join these spending-class participants in basic human progress?"

"I'll guess they are going to need a lot more cars."

"What is the implication of that for oil? Food? The comforts of life? You can apply that migration to anything you want, but just make sure you also apply it to the 'stuff' needed to make it all work."

"Which, in the case of an automobile, is an average of fifty pounds of copper."

"Bingo, Doc. Now let's hit the hotel and then we'll tackle the streets of Guangzhou."

***

After another half hour of driving through even more massive highway loops and clogged byways, we arrived in a secluded little neighborhood that was filled with bustling cafés, chic-looking lounges and otherwise nondescript office complexes. After dropping off our compact luggage kits at the hotel, I was already thankful I didn't have to drag that widowmaker around. We then hopped down to a nearby restaurant to get some grub and enjoy the atmosphere. Tomorrow we were taking the train from Guangzhou to Hubei province, where we'd go check out the Three Gorges Dam, so some respite was in order.

Right down to the tight jeans and weird haircuts, the restaurant we were eating at was eerily reminiscent of the bar we went to back home, where Johnny and I first started talking about trends.

"I didn't know they had so many funky folks in China, Johnny. You sure do have a knack for finding these kind of places."

"They got everything we got, only way more of it as you can expect in a city of twenty million."

"I mean, it's just fascinating to witness how alike these young people are to the kids in any American shopping mall. They dress alike, they act alike, I suppose they even read the same fashion blogs, it's quite remarkable, really."

"Wow Doc, fashion blogs? I'm surprised you even knew those existed. You really have come a long way. Just think, twenty years ago, none of this was here. But look a little deeper and you'll notice something else going on that sets them apart from their American doppelgangers. "

I looked across the room examining each patron from the shoes up. They definitely paid a lot more for their jeans than I did, and appeared even more obsessed with their smartphones than their American counterparts.

"Oh wise one, I give up, please enlighten me," I said.

Johnny pointed at a group of young ladies sitting at the bar and asked, "You see those girls? Look at their handbags. Those aren't knock-offs, they are genuine Fendis. Or how about the guy sitting at the table over there? Check out his watch."

"So they're rich kids?"

"Westerners aren't uniquely equipped at being the only people who are able to generate wealth, Doc. If you took a world tour four or five hundred years ago you may not have been that impressed with European cities and the American Colonies, however, you would surely have been blown away with the Far East as many a European trader was. We were just in the right place at the right time for our industrial revolutions while Asia was taking a nap sorting itself out. China's spending class of four hundred million and growing is experiencing a consumer mania of luxury goods."

"What kind of luxury goods?"

"You name it, they buy it. The Chinese addiction to luxury brands started out with the über-rich in the cosmopolitan neighborhoods of Shanghai and Beijing, but now the trend has gone nationwide. Designer brands are even setting up shop in China's third tier cities, something you don't see in Milwaukee or Toledo."

"Is there really that much demand?" I asked.

"There's so much interest in designer goods here that they've started opening up shopping malls that exclusively stock luxury brands. Some analysts are predicting that China will eclipse every other major market by a quantum for luxury goods. But right now, it's more about claiming space for the future than profiting today."

"How so?"

"If you build it, they will come. If you want to understand anything about China, you need to memorize that line like a Buddhist mantra. It can be applied to infrastructure, real estate and even expensive handbags. Brands like Louis Vuitton and Gucci know that China will continue to be their most important growth market. So in the meantime, they'll open stores across the country and rent space in these luxury malls even if they aren't profitable, just to have a presence."

"That's very interesting but it also sounds like the boutique version of the ghost cities we always hear about."

"It's all psychology, Doc."

"How so, you mean these guys are getting brainwashed?"

"The fact that so many western analysts and journalists are still wringing their hands over ghost cities or ghost malls or ghost anything, is, to use the language of your profession, a symptom of something entirely unrelated to the medium and long term planning of China's *planned* economy."

"It's a communist country and they do have something called five-year plans, Johnny."

"Exactly. Growth could never stay at 10% or 12% in perpetuity could it? What is frequently forgotten by the reporters and analysts is the base is getting bigger. Remember the overall economy grew by almost 10% for thirty years, the base is now a monster, second only to the United States so 7% or 8% growth is still a bigger number than 10% growth to the economy of ten years ago."

"Alright, if we're playing doctor, what's your diagnosis regarding how westerners see China?"

"The Chinese are speculators and a speculator is inherently optimistic about the future, while we westerners have become pessimistic after decades of stagnation. Most folks back home simply have forgotten what it is like to see your salary double every five or six years. Look back at the America of 50 and 100 years ago, with the exuberance in building the country with our super projects, the same thing the Chinese are doing now."

"You already told me that when America invested 4% or more of GDP into infrastructure the American economy grew by roughly the same rate, same as the Chinese economy has mirrored the 8% or 9% of GDP they have been investing into building. You're saying this is a matter of perception?"

"Definitely. Perception is the fundamental difference between the east and west, and it's the fundamental difference between being passive and being a participant. As J.M. Keynes said: Investing is an activity of forecasting the yield over the life of the asset; speculation is the activity of forecasting the psychology of the market."

"So if we go to one of these luxury shopping malls, and there's no customers, that's still a good thing? Those companies are speculating that it will get stronger in the future?"

"In my opinion these projects are a form of infrastructure – the infrastructure of consumerism. Another problem with the West's perception of the Chinese economic miracle is that we think it of it like it was a one-off event, rather than an ongoing process. A generation ago nobody here was even thinking of buying their first car, let alone splurging on designer clothes or expensive wine, another mania in China. Now millions have bought their first car, and we're sitting in a lounge filled with youth wearing designer brands. Yet it's still just a drop in the bucket of what will happen as another 500 million people join the spending class and gradually become bona fide consumers. The ongoing migration from rural to urban continues to be just the first step, now China is working on building the world's next great consumer society."

We chowed down some dumplings, had a few bottles of Tsing Tao while I mulled this over. After paying the bill, we hit the street and walked by a string of vendors haggling with would-be patrons. Then we passed a string of storefronts bustling with shoppers and young people who were spilling out of one bar to cross the street to the next. There were also quite a few expats who crossed our path, a high percentage of which were African, something else I didn't expect.

"I didn't expect it to be so diverse," I said as we cruised back towards the hotel.

"There's probably 60,000 expats here, half of which are African."

"Why is that?"

"It's the Chinese dream, Doc. We always hear about how hungry China is for African resources, well, Africa is equally hungry for Chinese goods and manufacturing techniques. Since the '90s, the keenest traders in countries like Nigeria realized they could cut out the middleman and come straight to where the 'stuff' they need is made to get it at the best price possible."

***

In just over a week we were going to travel cross-country from Guangzhou to Beijing, so our itinerary demanded an early rise, which meant lots of coffee. I wanted to see if I could find a typical local café in the neighborhood before we left, but was only able to find a Starbucks. To think that when they first started to crop up in Seattle I thought it was an idiotic trend that would never last. That's one of the stocks that got away.

Next on our list was the Three Gorges Dam, and to get there from Guangzhou, we needed to take a series of trains. I had ridden Amtrak a number of times in the past, but it had been at least ten years since I had last been subjected to rail travel. My experience with Amtrak had always been challenging, to put it nicely – cross-country trains were late, stalled, cramped and very slow. The sight of the train station gave me flashbacks of one very bitter Christmas Eve spent stranded in Boston due to a malfunctioning snowplow.

But after arriving at the Guangzhou station yesterday, I'd come to expect that every form of transport we would come across in China would be brand spanking new, and the bullet train we took on the first stretch of the trip did not disappoint. Not only was the train itself a gleaming space-age marvel, but the entire rail network seemed like it had been built the week before I arrived. In the course of five years, China's high-speed network had grown bigger than all of Europe's, now stretching more than 10,000 kilometers linking more than 11 cities – China uses the metric system, just like Europe and most of the world. I thought about that cold night in Boston and was supremely envious of the Chinese – a sensation I never would have predicted I'd ever have to suffer through. When one travels by train from Boston to New York it's like setting your watch back 75 years as the click-clack of our slow and antiquated railroad system echoes the need for a complete reset button to be pressed on so much of our ailing infrastructure.

In just five hours we travelled 900 kilometers, passing through Shaoguan, Zhuzhou, Changsha, Xianning, and a whole bunch more I wouldn't dare try to pronounce. A modern cross-country train ride in most other parts of world must be similar to what I experienced. The food, however, which was served from the usual rolling cart, was not at all typical: The offerings ranged from chicken beaks and gizzards to pig feet. My personal favorite from this exotic, yet intimidating, selection was pig's ears. All these delectables were neatly vacuumed packed with little clear windows letting you know what you were about to enjoy. Check please!

I knew about Shanghai and Beijing, and now Guangzhou, but had never heard of any of these other cities, and all of them had millions of inhabitants. It was simply amazing. It made sense to travel by train as it allowed us to observe the landscape in its entirety. If we had flown between our destinations, easily doable with the numerous modern airports built in past years, we never would have experienced the vast changes in landscape and culture. These cities were only going to get bigger, and the building blocks were in place to make it happen.

We arrived at Wuhan main train station, one of three in the city, to discover that it would take a bit longer to get to the dam than expected, so we decided to go off schedule and spend the night. It was another city that I, and likely no one back home, had ever heard of. Wuhan, a city of over ten million people, was like the Chicago of China because of the amount of expressways and rail lines that passed through it. Like Guangzhou, they also made a lot of cars there, and all the big names like Nissan, Hyundai, GM, Volkswagen, etc., had set up shop here, culminating in a production capacity that would likely break three million vehicles in the near future, earning the city the nickname "China's Detroit", because it would soon surpass the motor city's output during its pinnacle years.

Around the corner from our hotel, we found a little ramshackle restaurant set up in an alley and grabbed a couple of stools. I say restaurant, but it was more of a laissez-faire food court where you could buy dishes from a variety of vendors. Fried frog on a stick was on the menu but I wasn't quite ready to test my stomach's mettle against such exotic street meat. One of the customers spoke some English, and he let us know that the city's specialty was hot and dry noodles, so we ordered two bowls. It turned out he was a taxi driver, and was very eager to tell us about how congested traffic in the city had become over the last few years due to all the new cars and construction.

Our speaking English, and obviously being foreigners, seemed to attract a small crowd. There was a real desire for anyone learning English to practice their newly-learned skills on some native speakers. Even speaking in broken sentences with a limited vocabulary, we were able to talk to them about their ambitions and goals. Some of them wanted to study in America while others were starting and growing their own businesses right there in Wuhan. But what they all had in common was a positive outlook on the future, feeling they would be wealthier and happier than their parents. And all of them wanted that to happen in China.

One neatly dressed woman in her late-twenties wanted to have a family, a boy and a girl, something not possible for the generation before her under China's notorious one-child policy. Due to falling birth rates and increasing resistance, the policy had been amended to enable families to have more children. I thought to myself, what is the implication of this policy when factored over a fifty-year time horizon?

***

After a couple of train transfers and a four-hour bus trip we arrived at the Three Gorges Dam "scenic area" which consisted of a few viewing platforms and a garden. The place was teeming with tourists, mostly Chinese, with the odd Westerner mixed in. Beyond the visitors snapping photos was the colossal dam: the largest concrete and steel structure in the world. Built over seventeen years by 40,000 workers, it was the most ambitious civil engineering feat I'd ever heard of. I was now staring at it in amazement.

"What do you think, Doc?"

"It's massive."

"One hundred years in the making, quite an accomplishment."

I'd read up on the facts about the project before we left the US, and they were astonishing – it cost $37 billion to build, and required the relocation of over a million people. The Three Gorges Dam has the world's largest instantaneous generating capacity of 22,500 megawatts, ten times the size of the Hoover Dam, and three times bigger than America's largest, the Grand Coulee Dam in Washington State. The 22,500 megawatts is enough to power four cities the size of Los Angeles. It consisted of 27 million cubic meters of concrete and enough steel to build 63 Eiffel Towers, but seeing it with my own eyes was very different from reading a fact sheet. The scale was magnificent, and the implications even more so.

"This is true base-load green energy, meaning it runs at full capacity 24 hours a day 7 days a week," Johnny said. "A commonly used alternative, coal generation, would require 31 million tonnes of coal to be burned per year to produce the same amount of electricity, meaning this dam is saving the world one hundred million tonnes of greenhouse gas emissions," Johnny said.

"I remember going to Hoover Dam when I was a kid with my parents," I replied. "There was something so optimistic about it: like it was a giant symbol of American exceptionalism."

"We don't make infrastructure investments like this anymore. There's too much partisan politics and far too much debt, not just back home but all over the developed world. Plus it sure does help when you have a country of engineers to successfully imagine and execute a project of this scope. We have countless bridges in desperate need of repair, our ports need expanding, our airports need modernizing, hell, many states and counties can barely fix their potholes. We've totally forgotten how critical infrastructure is to a growing economy, and meanwhile, China continues to spend 8% of its GDP on projects like this."

"We used to have the capital and the know-how, now they have the capital and they already know how!" I joked to myself.

"Newspapers love to predict the impending collapse of China's economy, but meanwhile the Chinese march forward, easily able to finance these big state projects."

"So how are you so confident that it will continue?" I asked.

"Look what happened to America's economy after the Hoover dam was built – it was followed by an era of unparalleled progress and growth. If you build it, they will come. If you build the world's largest hydroelectric dam, there is a reason: it's because you know consumption of electricity since the invention of the light bulb has done nothing but increase. What are the better choices for reliable base load power needed to feed over one billion people?"

Solar power and wind power, great as complimentary power sources, simply did not have the scale for 24/7 reliability. The alternatives – coal, oil or natural gas – that will certainly be aided by the Russian-Chinese natural gas pipeline being built, all come with the negative side effects of carbon emissions. The other zero-emission source, nuclear, had its own controversial pros and cons. What was clear is that the 2.5 billion people of CHINDIA would need enormous amounts of electricity and it seemed like a better solution for it to come in the form of the Three Gorges Dam rather than polluting fossil fuels.

The final thought we were left with during our Three Gorges field visit was the added benefit of flood control. The guide had mentioned that over the decades hundreds of thousands of lives had been lost and tens of millions left homeless due to the unpredictable nature of the mighty Yangtze River, the longest in Asia.

***

In the morning, we got back on the bullet train and were in Shanghai, the most European city in China, by early afternoon. I was still blown away by the size and speed of the rail system, imagining what it would be like if I could hop on a train in Los Angeles and be in San Francisco within a few hours.

In contrast to Guangzhou and Wuhan, Shanghai seemed less like an industrial town and was more flamboyantly prosperous. Walking down the streets you could sense that this was a real seat of economic power. It was glossy, shiny, and felt successful. I couldn't help but notice how many art galleries and symbols of global culture there were as we worked our way through a series of vibrant neighborhoods towards Pudong, an area full of new skyscrapers.

We walked the length of the Bund on a riverside stroll with turn of the century European buildings echoing those of Paris and Vienna, juxtaposed against the glass giants across the river in Pudong.

Later that evening Sparky took me through a very hip neighbourhood, Xin Tian Di, where a smorgasbord of expats, locals and tourists, wined, dined and shopped themselves into oblivion. At my request, Sparky lead me to what one of the top fashion blogs had called the best wine and spirits bar in China - a stunning venue nestled in a beautiful building with a gleaming star-studded constellation logo beckoning revellers. Inside I witnessed a similar scene to that in Guangzhou - young, affluent youth clad in the latest fashions, texting away like mad on their smartphones. All this happening while quaffing single malt scotch and fine wines, both the top French and Italian labels and more recognizable wines from the US. This was a veritable shrine for the city's young, newfound wealth.

Shanghai's population was 24 million, making it the largest city by population in the world. When you think of the supercities like Tokyo, Moscow, Mexico City and New York, it's hard to imagine a place with more possibility than Shanghai. It is little wonder so many Chinese-born US university graduates come back to stake their claim on the future right here.

One day and night in Shanghai was far too short to appreciate all she had to offer but the show needed to get back on the road, the railroad that is. And as I quickly learned, the most prestigious rail link between any two cities in the world surely had to be the super train between Shanghai and Beijing.

"My first trip over here we took the 'old' train that *only* did 200 kilometers per hour. It took twelve hours door to door. For our trip today we will be riding on the fastest scheduled train in the world where we average 300 kilometers per hour and we'll be door to door, 1,300 kilometers, in only five hours."

"Five hours at 300km? That would be like traveling from Washington, DC to Miami in the same time, or Boston to New York in about 75 minutes!" I quickly calculated.

We scheduled the morning train so we could have true daylight for the whole voyage. Like the previous train rides, there was endless progress on both sides of the tracks. We passed these massive blocks of apartment housing 30 or 40 units wide and dozens of buildings thick; perhaps they were some of the ghost cities I had heard so much about. In Beijing I wanted to find out.

Taking that morning train enabled us to arrive just after lunch and enjoy an early afternoon walk. I began to understand what the maven meant when he talked about the Airpocalypse – the thick, steely-gray, smog made it difficult to see skyscrapers in the distance. While smog was prevalent in other areas we visited, it was noticeably worse here in Beijing. Everywhere people were wearing face masks, which had me self-consciously worry for my lungs.

We walked through a minefield of leisurely shoppers, stalls and stands selling everything from tourist kitsch to bizarre electronic innovations like a cellphone that doubled as a cigarette holder. Johnny taught me my first bit of Mandarin: "Bu Yao" meaning "don't want," which, when used repeatedly, was effective at keeping the hawkers at bay.

"Should I have brought a surgical mask, or an oxygen tank? The locals seem to be protecting their lungs from all this smog."

"Nah, you'll be fine Doc, just don't breathe too deeply."

"Well, that's reassuring."

"You should love this, it's a dream come true for a greenie like you!"

"How on God's green earth is walking through toxic smog fumes a dream?"

"Because it's conditions like these that are going to make China kick start the whole green economy into warp speed. This level of pollution is already uninhabitable and if they don't do something about it there will be more than just health issues to deal with. Like the saying goes, 'in every crisis there's an opportunity.' The Chinese government is already making cleaner air a priority and green tech innovation will be a pillar of their future economy, which means better, cheaper, green tech for the entire world."

"So what's happening with solar power, for instance, is going to happen to other green tech ideas?"

"You betcha. What they did for hydroelectricity in the south, they'll do for wind power in the north. China's installed capacity of wind power will more than double as they make the single biggest push in renewable energy in the coming years. That means they will have more investment in renewables than the United States and the European Community combined."

"That's a lot of windmills," I said.

"And with a lot of windmills comes ..."

"A lot of copper," I interrupted.

"Each windmill is its own self-contained power plant that has to be multiplied over and over instead of giant projects where backbone items are not repeated. Protection against lightning strikes, power distribution, and so on means more copper per kilowatt generated by a power of magnitude. Whenever you see a wind turbine, whisper that to yourself."

The contemporary industrial revolution I had witnessed over the past week was the fastest in history. According to Johnny, in only thirty years, China had gone from backwater to superpower, from little overall economic footprint to being the largest consumer of almost every major commodity.

Yet people are skeptical of the sustainability. On Henry Kissinger's 1971 visit to China he asked Zhou Enlai, Mao's foreign minister at the time, his assessment of the French Revolution. Zhou replied; "it's too early to say." The Chinese have always taken long and calculated steps so the full consequences of the thirty-year industrial revolution to date are also "to early to say."

After strolling past some of the more touristy spots of the city center we took a bus to Badaling, a nearby section of the Great Wall of China. Visually, it was even more astonishing than the Three Gorges Dam, but for an entirely different reason. As far as I could see there was an uninterrupted stream of people cascading through the wall's concourse, it was a sight to behold and a picture in a book could never capture this moment.

"My God," I said. "This place is packed like a college football game."

"Chinese tourists." Johnny said. "The world's most profitable renewable resource. Anyone feeling bearish about the Chinese economy should really just look at how much they are spending on their holidays."

"I'm guessing it's a lot?"

"One in ten global tourists is now Chinese. There are now almost 100 million outward-bound trips, half of which are for holidays or leisure. Which means Chinese tourists now spend more money worldwide than Americans. But here's the important part – 80% of these tourists say that shopping is the main reason for their trip. And guess how many Chinese have passports."

"Not many?"

"Just 5%. They spend nearly $150 billion around the world, and it's only at 5%. That's going to double in the next few years, and when that happens, the world will need to be prepared. Chinese tourism is a huge opportunity for any country wise enough to adopt the policies to encourage it. I hope the US will be one of them."

Tourism, that bastion of freedom we have had in America since our country was founded... even though I had the ability to travel all of these years I had been nowhere and seen nothing. All of a sudden going to Las Vegas or Miami Beach seemed far less exotic than what was really out there. My passport was going to get lots of mileage before it expired: This trip was the first of many and I was sure I would be running into lots of camera-carrying people from the Red Dragon.

***

On the last day of our trip, Johnny and I separated because he had meetings to attend with a mining firm he had invested in. So I had Beijing all to myself.

I did a quick tour of the city's architectural marvels, most of which didn't exist ten years ago. The National Stadium, or "Bird's Nest", was the largest steel structure on earth. While the Bird's Nest was impressive for its sheer size, I preferred the Galaxy Soho complex. Built in 2012 by the apparently renowned architect Zaha Hadid, it was a gigantic aluminum mega-mall that was home to some 370,000 square feet of commercial space. From a distance it looked like some futuristic alien spacecraft, something that would be very hard to get approved, or financed, in most parts of the world.

Walking through its cavernous interior, I couldn't help but be reminded of the Great Wall. It was obvious to anyone that the Chinese had a unique ability to plan on a grand scale and execute construction of their gargantuan dreams. They have the ability to build right here and right now without consideration for NIMBY, let alone BANANA issues.

Visually, the two structures couldn't be more different – one was a giant temple of consumerism, awaiting the world's next great consumer society to materialize, and the other was a man-made object visible from space, built to defend from raiding bandits.

But at their core, they were both grounded in the philosophy of 'build first,' a philosophy the Chinese had been employing for centuries. It turned out the Great Wall was a great idea: It allowed the Chinese empire to exist and flourish, and I got the feeling that this great mall would end up playing a similar role for the China of tomorrow.

I now considered myself to be a quasi-expert on emerging markets and their new spending-class consumers. On my flight home it was an especially nice feeling to be bumped up to business class as I boarded the plane for Seattle. Sitting next to me was a tidy looking fellow in a slim cut business suit.

"How's it going?" I asked.

"Tired, another long trip for only two days of meetings," he sombrely replied.

"You were here on business?"

"Yup, I come every two months or so, but always for a 48-hour power session. How about you?"

"I was here doing research on a financial soap opera."

"You're an actor?"

"No, I just follow financial markets like someone might follow Days of Our Lives, you know one of those daytime soap operas."

"Oh cool, what kind of markets are you in? I'm an investment banker specializing in clean-tech."

"So you know a thing or two about green energy?" I said, thinking to myself that this 14-hour flight was going to fly by.

"I know enough to be dangerous."

"What are your thoughts on commodities as *the* lynchpin for green energy?"

"Friend, let me tell you, the most important thing for green energy, is green money!"

"Really?"

"How do you think they make this stuff? With good old fashioned cash and a brilliant R&D department."

"Well we're gonna have some time between here and Seattle. Let me tell you about the green metal..."

11

Awakenings

Wednesdays were different now. They were still my favorite day of the week, but for an entirely new set of reasons. My daily ritual started with tending the garden I'd planted in my backyard. Once an overgrown patch of crabgrass, it was now overflowing with vegetables and herbs. Today I was particularly concerned with the progress of my tomato vine, which I had high hopes for.

I no longer wasted my mornings trying to find a parking spot for the Lincoln, because the Lincoln was long gone. I'd finally put my money where my mouth was and decided to buy an electric car – a BMW i3 to be exact. It was as eco-friendly as a vehicle could get and the slickest thing my neighborhood had ever seen.

Of course, I had installed a set of solar panels on the top of my garage some time ago, and that also offset my carbon footprint. It was a beautiful piece of engineering and had put my entire recent education into perspective.

There were over 450 pounds of batteries in the i3, no steel because it was made of carbon fiber and aluminum. It had a range of about 160 kilometers, which equals 100 miles for the non-metric folks, due to its 20 kilowatts of battery storage. The solar option with full sunlight operated at 3.5 kilowatt hours so it took five or six hours to fully charge. Since I lived in the predominantly overcast Pacific Northwest I also chose to install a supercharger that was hard-wired to my home so I can charge and go as much as I pleased, no matter what the weather was, in less than an hour. Even though the car was fully electric and I had the solar option, this supercharger was now the single biggest power draw in my home. You don't even want to know how much copper was used between the car, the batteries and all the cabling to make it possible. Thinking about it made me glad I now had exposure to copper as an investor.

'El Grande' was still there, but I was nearly at the summit. Everything electronic was automated and linked to my iPad and iPhone – lights, heating, entertainment system, the entire home was now space-aged. The bathrooms were still only half-done, but the remaining work was purely cosmetic, so I wasn't losing any sleep over an exposed pipe or two.

When I was done tending to the crops I usually settled into my home office, flipped open my laptop, and began to read my newsletters. Two of them would appear in my inbox by the time I'd poured my first cup of coffee. After returning from China, my first order of business had been to find another doctor who was willing to share my practice with me. It was a big decision, but the trip had tipped the scales. I didn't want to be one of those dusty old family doctors working well into his seventies, and if I was going to become a participant, a true blue contrarian investor, I knew I would need more free time to follow my financial soap operas.

Luckily, I found a young buck named Vijay, fresh out of his practicum, and brought him on board. He had a calm and pleasant bedside manner, and most importantly, he was an ardent Mariners fan. He was able to fit in right off the bat, so I was more than comfortable to leave him in charge for half the week.

It was also convenient that Vijay was raised in Mumbai, India, which was my next major project as I dissected the potential of the other end of CHINDIA. China had opened my eyes, but our quickly changing world also included India, Thailand, Indonesia and the whole African continent.

I salivated when thinking of the pages of my passport filling up with entry stamps. Vijay would be able to coach me through India, and the rest I would try to figure out along the way.

My second order of business after getting back was to stop using my online broker account for all of my investments and find a full-service stockbroker who was an expert on the things the new spending class wanted to buy. On Johnny's advice I took a trip to Vancouver and met with a close friend of his who had proven connections and a solid reputation. Everyone called him the "Birdman," for reasons I still don't understand, but it was likely due to his owl-like wisdom.

The first thing we did after discussing my investment goals was to restructure only a portion of my portfolio for "higher risk" opportunities. I still had Microsoft and Coca-Cola, but instead of chasing 8% with all of my investment dollars, I switched to a regimen wherein I'd put small percentages of my available funds into stocks related to my main financial soap operas: The ascent of man, of course, and the one I was most keen on – the greening of our planet with copper played a starring role.

Over and above some really good ideas and quick execution, an added advantage I had by using the Birdman's connections had been the access to private placements and exclusive initial public offerings and new stock issuances. The benefit of investing this way was the warrant to purchase additional shares in the future, which meant that I, the investor, had the right, but not the obligation, to buy additional shares – two, three or even five years into the future, and near the entry price level. This was the ultimate call on the future and my online account could never offer me that. Plus I had full access to the best and brightest minds in the research departments offering everything from bottom up company analysis to 40,000 foot macroeconomic views.

As far as choosing my master themes, the trip had taught me one unassailable truth: Nothing was going to stop China from eventually becoming the world's largest consumer society, it's simple arithmetic. The peasant who became the factory worker would soon become the shopper, and the same process was going to repeat itself across the globe with the next five hundred million, even one billion people. They all wanted to join in the basic economic progress that had allowed me to live such a great life. All those people wanted and deserved the same things as Americans, and there was no army, no government and no spiritual force that could hold them back.

And right down to the second, the front door opened and in walked Johnny for the favorite part of my Wednesday routine: our weekly briefing.

"Ok Doc, you said you had a hot tip for me today so it better be good," he said as he poured himself a cup of coffee.

"I was going to send it to you by e-mail but then I thought why don't I just write it down for you."

"Another research report to dissect?"

"Better still, I've decided to give my kids an education they can put to use. I've come up with Doc Copper's ten things every modern investor should know."

"You going to write them down? Maybe we should frame them next to the top five that changed my life?"

"That's a great idea, I was also going to put them in my office! Number one, if you pay peanuts you get monkeys. Number two, get a passport. Number three, the greener and cleaner we create energy..."

"The more that is demanded of copper. That's my line Doc!"

THE END

Afterword - About The Cover

I could not close-off *My Electrician Drives A Porsche?* without commenting on the cover of the book. Designed by my close friend, Vancouver-based artist Graeme Berglund, the cover's image is sure to spark more than a few thoughts and opinions.

Firstly, what does a title referencing a sports-car-driving electrician have anything to do with an American penny stamped into the geographic shape of China? The obvious answer, for those who want to cheat by not reading the book first, is the directly proportional relationship between China's rampant urbanization and her insatiable appetite for the world's natural resources, particularly the king of the industrial metals, copper.

There is, however, the additional reference of the text stamped on that famous American icon, "In God We Trust", as well as "Liberty" which were purposefully re-assembled as "Liberty In Rust", the title of Graeme's original art piece.

For most of the twentieth century, when the American Republic invested in excess of 4% of GDP on infrastructure, its economy grew in robust fashion and it led the world in almost every economic category. In more recent times that investment has shrunk to 2% of GDP or less, while expensive wars have been waged and costly crises addressed.

In Asia, and other parts of the developing world, investment into the building blocks of their economies has been 8%, 9%, or more of GDP, and we have all been witness to the impact of this breathtaking growth. The contemporary argument is that there has been too much development, particularly in China's real-estate market. Will a painful hangover need to occur to mop up the excess, leaving an ongoing drag, specifically on future demand for commodities?

That brings us back to the image, commissioned to symbolize the participants of human progress, and all that makes it possible. Unless people have extensively travelled the world, both east and west, they cannot have a truly balanced perspective of where we currently stand. Suggesting that America's infrastructure is rusting away, saddled by trillions of dollars of debt -- owed in most part to China, which continues to reinvest in seemingly unstoppable urbanization -- is simply a fair representation of the facts.

But here is the good news. The greatest example of un-biased wealth creation in history has been the American experience and this exceptionalism will yet again enable themselves to be reinvented. Jokingly, I once asked a mathematical whiz kid what the value of the United States was; that means every road, every bridge, every building,